Narrating Postmodern Time and Space

Narrating Postmodern Time and Space

Joseph Francese

State University of New York Press

Published by
State University of New York Press, Albany

Printed in the United States of America

For information, address State University of New York Press, State University Plaza, Albany, N.Y., 12246

Production by Diane Ganeles
Marketing by Dana Yanulavich

Library of Congress Cataloging-in-Publication Data

Francese, Joseph.
Narrating postmodern time and space / Joseph Francese.
p. cm. —
Includes bibliographical references and index.
ISBN 0-7914-3513-X (acid-free paper). — ISBN 0-7914-3514-8 (pbk. : acid-free paper)
1. Literature, Modern—20th century—History and criticism.
2. Postmodernism (Literature) I. Title.
PN771.F68 1997
809′.9113—dc21 96-51476
CIP

10 9 8 7 6 5 4 3 2 1

To Gina, with love

Contents

Abbreviations

Cc = *Le cosmicomiche*
Cds = *Collezione di sabbia*
Cvn = *Cosmicomiche vecchie e nuove*
Mm = *La memoria del mondo*
Ups = *Una pietra sopra*

1 Shifts and Imbrications

I. Interrogating the Postmodern

What points of orientation can help us understand contemporary history? In the humanities many commentators who treat our common condition of postmodernity begin with recent social and economic developments, and then compare and contrast the present intellectual climate to the modernism out of which it grew. Clearly, there are never distinct lines of demarcation between any two historical periods. In fact, the very concepts of modernity and postmodernity for Bauman are "important first and foremost (perhaps even solely) in the context of the self-awareness of the intellectuals, and in relation to the way the intellectuals perceive their social location, task and strategy" (227).

Nonetheless, modernity can be broadly, and very succinctly, defined as the evolution of structures of lived realities, such as subjectivity and identity. It is triggered by modernization, a term that denotes the changing modes of production and of distribution, and of new consumption practices consequent to the industrial revolution. Postmodernity, then, refers to the dramatic acceleration of the reshaping of structures of experience precipitated by the extremely rapid advances in information technologies during the past twenty-five years. Thus, making sense of the present and arriving at a modus vivendi within the continuous flow of postmodernity is an arduous task made even more formidable by the difficulty of gaining perspective on the time in which we live and the continuing transformation of our means of appropriating reality.

As Harvey has demonstrated, the revolution during the past quarter century in telecommunications has had a profound influence on the social and cultural organization of the industrialized West. Progress in the sciences has provoked some very dramatic alterations in the organization of capitalism. Rapid improvements in information technology have made possible the switch in the basic production mode from the fixed, Fordist assembly line to one of flexible accumulation, the disarticulation and displacement of capital and production to points all over the earth. The reorganization and globalization of the economy have in turn brought into being a shared condition of postmodernity characterized by modifications in real living conditions and of commonsense conceptions of space and time.

The globalized economy, heralded in the press by the incorporation of ever-larger supranational trading blocs, has abrogated the relative autonomy of social relations and of community inside traditional territorial boundaries, absorbing them into a global village. At the same time, traditional class distinctions within those national boundaries have also been supplanted, to some extent, by the postmodern division of the world into developing, proletarian nations, and bourgeois national economies increasingly based in the tertiary. More importantly, the subject of postmodernity is stripped of a traditional sense of place by postindustrial capitalism's ability to quickly relocate people and investments. Today the work place is a site of rapid change, flux, and uncertainty, where worker apprehensions are heightened by the volatility of markets and rapid shifts in consumption practices. They are compounded by the geographical mobility now forced on them and their families by the new, more flexible labor processes (Harvey 124).

The alienated, migrating worker of modernity has metamorphosed into its postmodern counterpart, who is fragmented by the loss of a sense of place and community. Workers are now faced with the dissolution of the traditional support system formerly provided by the extended and nuclear family. The weakening of the sense of belonging to a collectivity has left the individual with little to mediate between innate desires and the laws and mores imposed from without. Consequently, the subject of postmodernity is spatially disoriented.

The other defining characteristic of our condition of postmodernity is the shortening of commonsense perceptions of time. The long pasts and futures of our ancestors have collapsed. The influence of the past (the weight of tradition) and of future expectations (because of the electronic speed with which meaningful decisions must be made) are weakened. The loss of temporal bearings supervenes the individual who is now made to live more intensively in the present: the present is all there is. On a less conscious plane, future expectations are lowered further by the angst suffered by the various "Me," "Now," and "X" generations who have had to learn to live with their repressed fears of a future that will be used up before it arrives—either by nuclear holocaust or by the damage perpetrated every day on the environment. The loss of a sense of living and participating in a historical continuity (delineated by traditional values and beliefs) and the collapse of future expectations define the continuous present installed in postmodernity.

The quick and pervasive changes in the material conditions of everyday life caused by the progress and extension of information technology and the move toward a global marketplace have provoked in Western intellectuals a feeling of disempowerment. There is "too much to know and comprehend" (Federman, *Critifiction*). Our single and collective inability to keep pace with, influence, or direct the course of events has given rise to a "feeling of anxiety, out-of-placeness [and] loss of direction," which, in Bauman's opinion, "constitutes the true referent of the concept of postmodernity" (225). There is also a tacit sentiment of disorientation (I will treat this in my discussion of Calvino) caused by an inability to cognitively dominate the myriad small narratives of the new protagonists who have forced themselves into our collective awareness.

Contemporaneously, a new world order erected on the rubble of the Warsaw Pact must be confronted. Its cultural essence is a phagocytic (Pasolini) American model whose financial well-being depends on its ability not only to export weapons systems but also consumer goods. Older civilizations subject themselves to a cultural hegemony born of a trademark imperialism that is not content to meet needs but must also create new consumerist wants.

Many analysts of the postmodern would have us believe that the legitimation of multiple small narratives is a valid means of resisting homologation of planetary proportions. Vattimo's "heterotopias" are a good example of this type of response. However, the dominant classes are globally organized and more than capable of intervening locally. Therefore, a "postmodern" lack of faith in metanarratives does not justify turning one's back on the general context in which the particular becomes an object of knowledge (Simpson). Syntheses of marginalized discourses (narrations of narrations, so to speak) is the necessary but largely missing element from much postmodernist theory. If empowerment and truly pluralistic democracies are among the goals of postmodernism, then a multiplicity of narrative points of view, able to resist and transform postmodernity, are imperative.

Harvey contends that modernism was characterized by its conviction that "understanding had to be constructed through the exploration of multiple perspectives." However, he is quick to add, it "took on multiple perspectivism and relativism as its epistemology for revealing what it still took to be the true nature of a unified, though complex, underlying reality" (30). Inherent in our condition of postmodernity is the proclivity to undermine modernism's faith in a unified reality. However, the deconstruction of dominant discourse must be more than an amalgam of individualistic and anarchistic acts of micropolitics that perpetuate and intensify the disempowerment of those who "subversively" interpret but do not transform at a macropolitical level. We must go at least one step further and challenge the status quo.

In literature, the limitation of one's efforts to the ludic (Ebert) or ironic parody of the canon through metafictional pastiche nullifies literature's ability to dialectically intervene in the course of history with its own authentic force. Metafiction reflects the fragmentation of postmodern life—but does not aspire to transform it.

Resistance narratives go beyond the simple mimesis of postmodernity and seek to oppose and redirect it. They suggest to their readers points of self-orientation outside postmodernity's compressed space-time coordinates. They enable the reader to critically rethink, outside the parameters of a single world economic system, possibilities for self-determination and self-realization. They restore more human dimensions to postmodern space and time, and permit readers to reorient themselves within them. Their rejection of modernism's faith in a unified reality constitutes an active refusal of the modernist desire to homologate, integrate, and dominate diversity.

Thus, if a polycentric postmodern alternative to the unifying view of modernism is to be promoted in literature, it is necessary to distinguish between two sharply different responses to the present. On the one hand, there is the metafictional retreat from the already subjectivized world of high modernism into an even more private bibliographic universe where the only point of view is that of the writing *I*. On the other hand, oppositional postmodern valorizations of multiple diversit*ies* do not give one perspective predominance over all others. Narratives that contest postmodernity valorize counterdiscourses which place the subject in historical and associational systems of interdependence. They shatter the isolation of the subject of modernity by providing temporal and social points of orientation.

Because of the ubiquitous and invasive nature of postmodernity, any attempt to comprehend a particular writer's place within it must look far beyond the specifically esthetic parameters of a text and consider the social, political, and economic factors that condition writer and work. To reiterate a founding notion of historicist criticism, one must enter into the "zone of mutual trangressions" between writer, text, critic, and society (Bennett 5). For this reason, the point of departure for my textual analyses is a study of the poetics (or, as Binni phrases it, the active consciousness of inspiration) of the authors treated in this book. This reading strategy envisions the text as an integral part of the historical context in which it first appeared and as it interacts today with a reader who is "firmly rooted in existence, [has] a history, a profession, a religion, and even reading experience" (Blanchot 194).

In the chapter dedicated to oppositional postmodern narratives, I use Benjaminian remembrance as a means of recuperating fragments of the past so that they may serve as a guide for praxis. Although the person of letters is often tempted to profess that all that remains of the past is conserved in texts, this is not always the case. In fact, the reinscription in the present of the detritus of history (for example, orally transmitted knowledge of the marginalized and memories repressed in the unconscious) causes the recovered past to dialectically interact with the present.

Thus, remembrance (the recuperation of a temporal depth lost to postmodernity) is a valid means for restoring fragmented electronic time and space to manageable parameters. Benjamin suggests a form of "dialectical thought" that reinserts in the present events written out of received grand narratives of history, which are grounded in a concatenation of causes and effects.[1] Benjaminian remembrance can be utilized as a first response to the abbreviated temporal horizons of postmodernity and its lost historical sequence.

With this in mind, we can begin to postulate criteria for distinguishing between modern and postmodern literature. According to many commentators, esthetic or ludic postmodernism—what I will argue is in fact a late form of literary modernism—is characterized by, among other things, self-reflexivity, irony, and parody. When these commonly cited stylistic traits—along with, for example, the mixture of high and low art, indeterminacy and contingency—become ends unto themselves, they prove to be nothing more than a purely formalistic, hence socially passive, reflection of the condition of postmodernity.

The work of John Barth and Calvino fit comfortably within such a description of esthetic postmodernism. Both use metafictional self-irony, but not to decenter the subject. In fact, when compared to that of the high modernists, their work further privatizes human experience and places the individual squarely at the center of a Ptolemaic universe. When we compare the late modernist writings of Calvino and Barth to the oppositional postmodernisms of Morrison, Doctorow, and Tabucchi, the irrelevance of stylistic criteria in establishing a line of demarcation between literary modernism and postmodernism is underscored.

II. Modern/Postmodern

In the chapters that follow I will demonstrate a viable working distinction between late modernist and postmodern fictions. To that end I compare and contrast the work of the mature Italo Calvino (1923–1985) and John Barth (b. 1930), whom I consider late modernists, to the oppositional postmodernisms of Toni Morrison (b. 1931), E.L. Doctorow (b. 1931), and Antonio Tabucchi (b. 1943). I argue that postmodern narratives do not use the writing subject as the organizing center of consciousness, a strategy characteristic of high literary modernism that also underpins the work of Barth and Calvino.

A significant part of this book will retrace the intellectual biography of a major author, Calvino, over the second half of his career, as it straddles the shift in literary sensibilities from the modern to the postmodern. A close reading of what he produced during the last two decades of his life will rebut the consensus among Calvino's English-language critics regarding the emblematically postmodern qualities of his writings. Calvino's popularity in the Anglophonic world makes his work a very convenient point of access and departure for a comparative study of American and Italian modern and postmodern writings. In addition, his career is in many respects representative of the second half of Italy's *Novecento*. Like the majority of intellectuals of his generation who came of age during the Resistance movement, Calvino felt he had to overcome the esthetic theories of the Idealist philosopher Benedetto Croce that had informed his youth. His first novels were inspired by Neorealism, the most important literary movement in Italy during the decade following the Second World War. Subsequently, he was one of the main protagonists of the deprovincialization of Italian letters and its integration into the European mainstream.

In the 1960s Calvino embraced French Structuralism and subsequently embarked on an epistemological project that questioned the foundations of perceived reality. During this period a gradual shift in focus occurs: his interrogation of the world forsakes the deductive reason of his youth in favor of an inductive approach. Then, roughly a decade before his death, he began to analyze the essence of specific microcosms so that he might discover a general theory of knowledge.

Because of his rejection of a predetermining cognitive model and ultimate perplexity or inability to elaborate a general system, critics such as JoAnn Cannon consider

Calvino a postmodern writer. However, I will contend that the goal of his examination of the particular was to abstract from what he had learned a foundational metanarrative capable of reconciling the myriad small narratives of postmodernity. A constant throughout this process of intellectual and artistic maturation and development, I would add parenthetically, was his modernist insistence on the writing subject as organizing center of consciousness. Thus, my reading of the work of the mature Calvino concentrates on how and why he perceived and interpreted differently during the last two decades of his career, how this modified perspective emanates from his writings, and the relationship between his personal growth as writer and thinker and our condition of postmodernity.

While any discussion of the postmodern must necessarily avoid privileging any one of many conflicting narratives, neither can the close examination of evolving microcosms, or "molecular movement" (Gramsci), be eluded. Rather, the reciprocal effects of the grand social, economic, and intellectual forces on a historically conditioned individual can and must be measured. This awareness motivates the intensity of focus given Calvino in this book.

My attention to the poetics of the American novelist John Barth will help define and clarify why I consider Calvino a late modernist. The juxtaposition is not coincidental: Barth and Calvino read and spoke approvingly of each other's work. Furthermore, my treatment of Barth underscores the radical subjectivity common to the metafictions of both writers, along with their explicit concern for the art and the act of creative writing and the belief they shared in a finite bibliographic universe which can be reconfigured in an infinite number of ways. In response to the postmodern undermining of all strong narratives, both Barth's and Calvino's individual brands of metafiction claim that the perspective of the author is deprivileged and that a more democratic polyphony of readers' responses is achieved when the author self-consciously writes about the act of writing. But,

create a "sharable world" in which her reader may participate. Tabucchi recuperates from the high modernist Pessoa a process of radical self-examination. However, he restores the subject of narrative to social consortium when he equates the internal other (the hidden, repressed aspects of the psyche) with what is other (everything that is alien and potentially hostile to the conscious ego). His dialogue with the repressed leads him to acknowledge the nonmonolithic nature of the writing I, and then, and more importantly, to acquire the self-knowledge that can be gained only through the interactive mediation of other individuals. This heightened self-awareness provides the basis for the reaffirmation of social bonds. Doctorow does not utilize multiple narrative perspectives. However, he questions the truth value of univocal historiographic representations when he undermines the testimony of his narrating persona and in so doing validates alternative readings of the past.

The composite description of oppositional postmodern subjects limned in the work of these three authors recuperates what was marginalized in the past and strives to overcome dialogically the alienation of the modernist subject and the fragmentation or schizophrenia of its present-day counterpart. It does so not by reverting unto itself, as is the case with high and late literary modernism, but by seeking out objectifying points of reference in what is other.

2 Calvino: The Search for a Totality

I. *"Il midollo del leone"*

It is a commonplace of Calvinian criticism to divide his career as a writer into two more or less equal parts, both lasting approximately twenty years. The period from 1945 until approximately 1965 is the period of his literary apprenticeship, his militancy in the Italian Communist Party—which included active participation in the Resistance movement during the war and collaboration with the Party newspaper as a culture critic and political journalist through the ensuing decade. Creatively, during this period Calvino juxtaposed a fablelike prose to works that incorporated elements of neorealist investigation.

The second decade of his career begins with his disillusionment and resignation from the Communist Party in 1957. This followed Kruschev's denunciation of Stalin, the Soviet invasions of its Warsaw Pact allies in the mid-1950s, and, to his mind, the Party's ambiguous and slow response to the events in Eastern Europe. The journalistic and theoretical essays produced during the decade successive to his resignation from the Italian Communist Party are indicative of his increasing independence from all literary groups and their journals, with the notable exception of those associated with the Einaudi publishing house—particularly Vittorini's *Il menabò* (Ferretti, *Le capre di Bikini* 49).

Calvino's distancing from contemporary social, cultural, and political events (Ferretti 96) coincides with the waning of a future-oriented project and the definitive eclipse of explicit social investigation in his prose. His cosmicomic stories of the mid- and late 1960s are indicative of his redimensioning of the human within a much broader spatial and temporal context and the intensification of his search for an origin. The ultimate perplexity of which Cannon has written is a result of Calvino's inability, in the face of the bottomless relativity of meaning, to unearth a bedrock of knowledge. Among those critics who discuss Calvino in the light of postmodernity, it is almost a given that the literary production of the last two decades of his career is emblematic of the postmodern literary season. For Dombroski "it would be hard to find a more paradigmatic text [than *Le città invisibili*] to illustrate the postmodern perspective in literature" (*Properties of Writing* 176). Cannon has called *Palomar* "not only a *summa* of Calvino's work but also a parable of the postmodern condition" (*Postmodern Italian Fiction* 96). This is undeniably true as far as Calvino's "incapacity to grasp the whole" led to an increased perplexity and weakening of a future-oriented social project.

However, Calvino does not willfully contest inherited intellectual constructs. His is a very passive postmodernity. As one continues to read the production of his later period, it becomes increasingly clear that the overriding tendency is not an attempt to undermine what, or how, we know, but to reaffirm a metadiscourse grounded in reason. The faith in rationality that distinguishes all of Calvino's work is shaken during the 1960s by the undoing of the certainties of his youth. Reason ceases to be a liberating force capable of reversing capitalist oppression of humanity and destruction of the environment. Contemporaneously, the assertion and articulation of new forces antithetical to capitalism, which expanded and superseded a traditional working-class definition, new Third World and feminist protagonists, for example, helped to create in Calvino the disorientation underscored by Cannon. Thus, although his writings utilize the stylistic trends of esthetic literary postmodernism and demonstrate a perplexity congruent with a "postmodern" *Zeitgeist*, underlying his prose is an epistemological project whose implied goal is to reaffirm enlightened reason.

Underpinning Calvino's literary and intellectual investigation prior to the mid-1960s was what Ferretti (borrowing the title of a well-known essay penned in 1955 by Calvino) has called the poetics of "*Il midollo del leone*," "the lion's marrow." The theoretical basis of this poetic is solidly entrenched within the Crocean tradition and centers on the moral subject who determines consciousness. That Calvino would frame the question in the Gramscian terms of "building a new intellectual for a new literature" (Ferretti 14) is symptomatic of the facile grafting of Gramscian thought onto Croce typical of many Leftist Italian intellectuals during the postwar years. However, what matters more is that, despite Calvino's statements to the contrary,[1] Croce's thought extended its latent presence well into the latter stages of his career. Calvino's identification of and reaction to the labyrinth in 1962 ("*Sfida al labirinto*" Ups 82–97) was consistent with the poetics first elaborated in 1955 which stressed the importance of the "moral personality" and reaffirmed his belief in the importance of working to reverse the fortunes of rational, human intelligence (Ups 15).

The Idealist philosopher Benedetto Croce exerted a pervasive cultural hegemony over Italian intellectual life throughout the first half of this century. Calvino and many of his contemporaries who came of age in the Resistance movement attempted to overcome their essentially Crocean intellectual formation in the immediate postwar period. More often than not—and this was certainly the case with Calvino—Croce's esthetics were repressed and denied, not superseded (see Luperini 374–75).

The "moral personality" that provides the foundation for programmatic essays such as "*Il midollo del leone*" is, in point of fact, recuperated from Croce. Significantly, while Calvino was willing to admit having taken from Croce lessons on moral stoicism, it comes as no surprise, given the intellectual climate of the time and his concern with his public image, that he would have us believe Croce's esthetics were alien to him (see Ups 49).

The poetics of "*Il midollo del leone*" is further developed in two major essays, "*Il mare dell'oggettività*" (1960) and "*L'antitesi operaia*" (1964). These center on the importance of safeguarding the moral individual against the rising tide of amoral objectivity—that is, of rapid industrialization and urbanization.

The illuministic faith in human reason of Calvino's youth was future-oriented. In the period coinciding with and subsequent to his literary debut, Calvino believed that his militancy in a mass workers' party would contribute to a process of social renewal whose end was a more just and rational human consortium. Furthermore, as Ferretti has convincingly argued, reason was to be used to effect the Enlightenment utopia of a cohesive reintegration of humankind into the natural environment. The abrupt deflation of the myth of Stalin was to be the first significant road mark in Calvino's intellectual journey. As explained after the fact by Calvino, his youthful infatuation with the "merciless logic" of Stalinism ("*Quel giorno i carri armati uccisero le nostre speranze*") was consistent with his intellectual formation. In his own words, the myth of Stalin "appeared as the point of arrival of the Enlightenment project to subject the entire mechanism of society to the domination of the intellect" ("*Sono stato stalinista anch'io?*").

The second half of Calvino's career is marked by his gradual detachment from society and politics. His last "engaged" novel, *La giornata di uno scrutatore* (1963), is followed by *Le cosmicomiche*, a book that marks the beginning of the second phase of his career and, therefore, the starting point for our analysis of the relative modernity or postmodernity of Calvino's mature work.

Calvino's distancing from the political arena coincided with the resurfacing of a deeply ingrained individualism, which led him to posit, in *Le cosmicomiche*, the subject as the only point of reference within the surrounding system of relativized space-time coordinates. His faith in the capability of reason to encyclopedically embrace the knowable caused him to place the subject at the center of all experience. The priority of the individual took various shapes over the second half of his career but was never overcome or discarded. In fact, through Qfwfq, he took pains to validate the human by paradoxically locating it within a grounding discourse of galactic or macroscopic dimensions. In the prehistoric origins of the cosmos and humanity, he hoped to find absolutes, a material referent and a bedrock for knowledge.

In the 1980s the Calvinian subject comes to contemplate microscopic aspects of an objective world that exists independently of the subject. His hope was to uncover the essence of subjectivity by going beyond subjectivity. However, Palomar's phenomenological "intercourse with the outside" will fall far short of what Merleau-Ponty calls "true communication," the establishment of a communicative relationship between perceiving subjects, because dialectic exchange with "other myselves" does not figure in Palomar's alienated ruminations. Thus, the relativity of the multitudinous *petits récits* of postmodernism are not a source of strength for Calvino. They are precisely what his subject-centric vision works to overcome.

During the last two decades of his life Calvino's literary investigation is a quest for a unifying discourse, an Ur-narrative, that would enable him to attain an encyclopedic, suprahistorical, nonanthropocentric point of reference. His cognitive mapping of a foundation for a totality of knowledge does not "move laterally" from one *petit récit* to another, but is decidely hierarchical. The patterns he sees and utilizes to construct a vision of reality privilege certain elements over others. As he says in *Collezione di sabbia*, it is a question of how we see and abstract—that is, of placing certain elements of observed reality into relief and others into the background, creating matrices, and then wresting meaning from those matrices (168).

Therefore, although his cosmicomic vision seemingly redimensions the primacy of the subject, he was in fact attempting to safeguard it through complete and total investment. Thus, Calvino's nonanthropocentric vision is a logical outgrowth, not an abjuration, of the poetics of *"Il midollo del leone."*

II. The "Turning Point"

After the crisis of 1956 there was within the Italian Left a general sense of disorientation. Contemporaneously, the void felt in literature by the eclipse of Neorealism, according to Asor Rosa, was filled by three distinct tendencies: the reformist tendency (of which Calvino was a prominent exponent), the neoavantgarde, and third, the revolutionary tendency. The writings of the Neoavantgarde (or as it called itself "Gruppo '63," after the date of its formal constitution) gave priority to linguistic questions over ideological ones. Loosely united, the Neoavantgarde was characterized perhaps more by disagreement than agreement on a common platform and by the refusal to conjoin literature and politics. It was considered successor to the historical avantgarde because of its rediscovery of the linguistic investigation characteristic of the latter movement.

The more politically radical or revolutionary literary movement, in Asor Rosa's view, arose after the "season of social crisis and worker contestations that inaugurated the early 1960s" (635). The writers and critics associated with this tendency spoke to "an 'intimate' politics which was not to be superimposed on works of literature" (635). With this stance they responded at least in part to the insistence on content over formal questions common to much Neorealist investigation.

Vittorini was the undisputed leader of the reformist trend. In Asor Rosa's recounting, it was defined by the belief that the role of literature was to enhance and deepen our knowledge of reality. *Il menabò della letteratura*, a literary review directed by Vittorini and Calvino, became "the most authoritative organ of this tendency to conceive of literary renewal in prevalently experimental and linguistic terms" (623). Noting Calvino's objection to the Neoavantgarde's refutation of reason, its having "shipwrecked in the sea of objectivity," and its unconditional surrender to the chaotic labyrinth of contemporary reality, Asor Rosa sees in Calvino's "*Il mare dell'oggettività*" (originally published in *Il menabò*) "a strong criticism of the desperation of the old and new avantgardes, whom Vittorini had already reproached for having ceased believing in their capability to transform culture" (627). Within this literary milieu Calvino began to write his Cosmicomic stories.

Critics of Calvino are in general agreement that a shift in narrative and epistemological focus can be ascertained in his writings of the mid–1960s. The various criteria used to differentiate between the first and second periods of his career revolve around his retreat from political engagement and the increasing emphasis on literature's cognitive potential. The move toward a suprahuman, nonanthropocentric perspective informs four collections of brief narrative commonly referred to as the cosmicomic stories, *Le cosmicomiche* (1965), *Ti con zero* (1967), *La memoria del mondo* (1968), and *Cosmicomiche vecchie e nuove* (1984). These books trace a pattern of development from a transitive, transformative concept of literature to one that is intransitive—in other words, social incisiveness is postponed until cognitive mastery of reality can be achieved. Thus, when critics such as Ahern and Ferretti read what Calvino produced in the mid- and late 1960s, they are primarily concerned with the redimensioning of Calvino's social commitment.

In contradistinction, those who consider the mature work of Calvino emblematic of the postmodern literary season concentrate on the combinatory play and epistemological relativism characteristic of the latter two decades of Calvino's career. All concur, however, that literature for Calvino comes to be less a catalyst and increasingly a passive recorder of phenomena. After this point in time Calvino will desist in his attempts to reconcile or reintegrate the individual into the collective, as was the case in the 1940s and 1950s. The retreat from the world will bring about a lack of dialogic points of reference that will in turn disorient the subject, depriving it of its transitivity.

For Ferretti, a constant of Calvino's work is the opposition of an indecipherable prerational or arational otherness of the natural and animal world to human order. Calvino's *progettualità*, or future-oriented critical-constructive tension, aimed at helping society overcome its atavistic insensitivity or senselessness (*insensatezza*) and irrational treatment of the natural world and hoped to spur humankind to work to reintegrate itself into its surroundings. By the mid-1960s, however, the "rightful assumption of responsability, the moral necessities of speaking out and of protagonism" met with a "disillusioned and disenchanted rationality" (54).

As time went on, Calvino's faith in reason's capacity to dominate history began to give way to an objectivity dominated by the flow of events (62). His belief in the possibility of somehow controlling or humanizing the labyrinth of phenomena with a rationality grounded in Marxism was supplanted by a vision of an *insensatezza* devoid of ideological and classist connotations (63–64). Beginning roughly in the mid-1960s, Calvino's *progettualità* reverses and reorients itself toward the past—specifically, the writer looks to reinvent and rewrite the events that determined and conditioned life in the present. The culmination of this process, in Ferretti's reading, is an ultimate surrender to the labyrinth (146–47).

My reading of Calvino owes a great deal to Ferretti's. My only significant disagreement with his analysis centers on his claim that Calvino's tendency to decompose totalities into multiplicities is a manifestation of a refusal of unifying interpretations, of global designs, of universal models on the one hand and, on the other hand, the equally tenacious valorization of limited moments, minute realities, and microhistories (143). The identification of an implicit insistence on a global project causes my reading of the mature Calvino to differ. It leads me to see Calvino's final works not as examples of postmodern prose, but rather as examples of late modernism.

The waning of Calvino's faith in the ability of the intellectual to understand and transform the future will be accompanied by his recuperation and emphasis of Roland Barthes's ideas regarding the centrality of the text, the "death of the author," and the transferral of responsibility for the creation of meaning to the reader. Consequently Calvino will begin to seek out a resolution predicated on the redimensioning of the subject. In *Le cosmicomiche* Calvino's gaze reverts to the origins of the cosmos and to a much broader, nonanthropocentric context. Paradoxically, the objectivity thus afforded reestablishes the primacy of the intellect, which creates reality by projecting onto the outside its own interior world.

Cannon looks not to a specific text but to Calvino's biography for the motive or catalyst for change in narrative focus. In her opinion the death in 1966 of Calvino's mentor, the writer Elio Vittorini, is the watershed event. She writes:

> After the mid-1960s, which marked the end of Calvino's collaboration with Vittorini, Calvino's essays deal less and less with the ethical dimension of literature and more with its cognitive potential. The notion of changing the world is deferred until such time as the writer finds the instruments to comprehend it." [*Postmodern Italian Fiction* 35]

Thus, "with each successive work of fiction [he] finds himself situated at a different point on a continuum that runs from the *conoscibilità del mondo* to absolute indeterminacy." As she writes elsewhere, the last two decades of

Calvino's career are characterized by "an increasing tension between his aspirations for his fiction and the fear that the longed-for conversion of writing and action, praxis and poiesis, is mere sleight of hand" ("Italo Calvino: The Last Two Decades" 51).

Cannon's thesis is substantiated by Calvino in an interview with the Italian author Ferdinando Camon. As Calvino noted, "the fact is that the years following his [Vittorini's] death I began to distance myself from things and events, to change my work rhythm" (190; see also D'Eramo 133).[2] The loss of faith in political engagement following Vittorini's death will be underscored once again in 1980 by Calvino in the "Presentation" to *Una pietra sopra*. There he wrote of the waning of any pretense he may have previously had of "interpreting and guiding a historical process" and the assertion of "a posture of systematic perplexity" (viii) that in his later years would subtend the projected construction of a grand design.

The demythification of Stalin and then the death of Vittorini prompted Calvino to gradually but never completely distance himself from politics. Then the acquisition of a phenomenological perspective reinforced the youthful tendency to view reality as relative to the perceiving subject. In addition, as we shall see, his interest in basic narrative units, crucial to his combinatoric experimentation of the early 1970s, extends backward in time at least to his work on the *Fiabe* in the mid 1950s. Thus, it is more exact to speak not of a turning point, but rather of a gradual shift in focus that is first evident in *Le cosmicomiche*.

III. Qfwfq

In *Le cosmicomiche* Qfwfq establishes space-time coordinates that authenticate his interpretation of material reality. The process by which external reality is intellectually constructed is contingent on the prior creation of subjectivity along lines that evoke Calvino's Crocean formation. In *Le cosmicomiche* consciousness informs reality, a totality of space/time coordinates relative to the individual. In turn, that reality returns through visual perception to dialectically interact with consciousness. Not only does the subject believe it exists because it thinks, but the existence of the material also is construed as dependent on the thinking subject. At the same time, writing—the external manifestation of that thinking subject—gives material proof of the individual's existence. Once externalized, it becomes part of the reality that reflects back on and interacts with consciousness through sight.

The infinite series of binary oppositions that succeeded each other to shape life on our planet are retraced in *Le cosmicomiche* back to the origin on which Calvino would ground his metanarrative. Given that every event in time determines all future possibilities, Calvino's strategy is to examine the mutually exclusive choices that have been made at an atomic and cellular level prior to the birth of humanity. This strategy is particularly evident in "*Quanto scommettiamo.*" Here the "logic of cybernetics" (the symmetric dichotomies on which these stories are thematically grounded) is used to retrace paths taken and not taken, the chain "retroactions," both postitive and negative, back to the origin of the universe (103). Qfwfq's pronostications use base-2, either/or, calculations to predict, as it were, "the intersection of space and time where events would spring up" (106).

The return to the origin of time implies an awareness that the history of matter is an ongoing rearrangement of a finite number of eternally present molecules, and of the infinite combinatoric potentialities within that determinate totality. This understanding in turn justifies the creation and self-authentication of the subject. "*La spirale,*" the final story collected in *Le cosmicomiche*, tells of an organism whose existence predates identity (Cc 169–70). From this very low rung on the ladder of evolution, the infinite possibilities of ulterior physiological development and history can be contemplated as they fan out into the future:

> Think of how she would be transformed from formlessness if she were to take on one of an infinite number of possible forms, remaining, thoughout this process, herself. In other words, I could not imagine the forms she might have taken, but I did contemplate the special qualities that she would give to those forms. [Cc 173–74][3]

This leads the narrating persona to project its identity onto the world outside through self-expression: the fabrication of a mollusk shell. The shell is the external, visual sign of an interior consciousness, or Crocean intuition, that exists independently of and prior to the creation of a material, visual image, the shell. Creation of the shell is a fundamental selection that allows this particular life-form to survive. Moreover, it determines all ensuing evolutionary choices as this species continues on its bifurcating way. More importantly, the existence of the other is established and validated by the external emanation of the subject's internal essence:

> In one way or another, the great revolution had taken place: all of a sudden eyes and corneas and irises and pupils opened up around us. . . . All of these eyes were mine. I had made them possible; I had played the active role; I provided the raw material, the image. Along with the eyes everything else came. Therefore, everything that the others, who had eyes, had become—their form and function, the sum of things they were able to do because they had eyes—was a consequence of what I had done. That is why they were implicit in my being there, in my relationships with others, et cetera, in my beginning to be a shell, et cetera. To make a long story short, I had foreseen everything. [Cc 183]

The shell is only a representation of "*la parte piú vera*" of the narrator's identity: it is at one remove from his essence. As Qfwfq recounts, the shell was, "unlike me . . . [it was] the explanation of who I was, my portrait transposed into a rhythmic system of volumes and colors and stripes and hard stuff" (176). In Crocean terminology, *la conchiglia* is not the esthetic fact but merely the artistic fact. For Croce history was mere content, raw material for the Spirit, a stimulus for artistic intuition, just as artistic form was no more than the externalization of intuition. The Spirit was realized in the esthetic fact, or intuition, a purely intellectual, suprahistorical activity. The esthetic fact existed independently of the artistic fact, the concrete, historical manifestation of intuition,[4] and was of primary concern.

For Croce the artistic fact was expended by critical reflection. Art was not to be subjected necessarily to contemplation but was to stimulate the intuitive understanding of the beholder/reader. Qfwfq's shell is first and foremost an emanation of consciousness. Moreover, since there is a plurality of observers, the visual image is a potentiality (the other must choose to observe it), subject to interpretation by the beholder. Significantly, the immanent narrator is sightless. His transformation into addressee of his own artistic message is precluded.

The visual image, the artistic expression of the creative consciousness, informs the consciousness of the observer ("I thought of the link between eye and enchepalon as a tunnel dug from the outside in by the force of what was ready to become image, not from the inside out by the intent to intercept any image" [Cc181]). Only after consciousness has informed reality can the latter structure the former.

The subject that observes the mollusk shell is a consciousness that, through a process similar to the one described by the immanent narrator, has constructed for itself an identity and a paradigm for interpreting reality prior to viewing Qfwfq's shell: "I lived behind each of those eyes, that is to say another me lived there, one of the many images of me" (184).

In *Un segno nello spazio*, writing—or to be more precise a graphic sign made by Qfwfq—is an emanation of consciousness and the first point of reference for all future intellectual constructs. The original mark Qfwfq traces in the galactic void is designated a sign because it can be recognized as such "without risk of error" (42). This outward emanation of internal consciousness is a manifestation of his *cogito*: in his words, "that was the first chance I ever had to think something" (43). This expression of the esthetic fact establishes his identity ("the sign, the point, that which made me . . . me") (45). It can now be contrasted to an-other ("space, without signs, was once again an empty chasm with no beginning or end, nauseating, in which everything—myself included—got lost" [45–46]). Identity, once constituted, permits the localization of exterior spatial coordinates. Through identity, reality is constructed and space is given shape: both are structured in relation to the subject. As Qfwfq asserts, "independently of signs, space did not exist and perhaps it had never existed" (51). The ability to create, distinguish, and interpret signs makes space exist for the self-generating and self-authenticating post-Crocean subject. This way of perceiving the world will be displaced by Calvino's acknowledgment of a universe that exists autonomously of the subject, what I will refer to as the Montalean void or Borgesean "Hidebehind."[5] However, at this point, space is not an objective entity for Qfwfq, but relative to the subject's location within it. The constitution of identity and consequently the ability to distinguish self from other (in this case Qfwfq from Ursula H'x and Fenimore) opens the door to the understanding that "space with something in it and empty space are not the same thing" (144). Subsequently, *la forma dello spazio* projected by the narrating *I* becomes "common sense" (137).

The demarcation of spatial coordinates relative to the subject makes possible the measurement of time. When Qfwfq is unable to identify spatial points of reference, he sees himself trapped in an "interminable present" ("*Il guida-*

tore notturno" 137). When space is nonexistent for the subject, so is time: in "*Tutto in un punto*," "neither a before nor an after nor an elsewhere existed" (56–57). In "*La distanza della Luna*," the narrative that opens the collection, the reification of subjective space and time has already taken place. When Qfwfq's space coordinates are rapidly changed (for example pages 21–22 he suddenly finds himself trapped on the moon), he is disoriented and is forced to rethink common sense. Thus, the consciousness that first informed reality, defined its own space/time coordinates, and then concealed their genesis, must now react to elements of disorder and adapt. Having established his subjectivity (I am, therefore I create space and time intellectually, therefore I write, as it were) he is empowered to perceive and then to construct a systematic knowledge of the external world.

Once Qfwfq has grounded all knowledge in his own subjectivity, he sets in motion a process of mystification that conceals the foundations of his epistemology. Qfwfq would have us believe that he must necessarily be able to perceive and distinguish what is other in order to define himself. He uses writing to reverse the roles of artificer and artifact and argues that he is the creation, not the creator, of his sign. When he asserts, "meanwhile, sight had come into our world and, as a consequence, life" (Cc 46), he reveals the inverted nature of his premise. After all, perception, not life, is contingent on sight. He thus attributes to a sign he has made an objective quality that leads him to distinguish it from a second, more subjective sign (also of his hand), hypostatizing the first.

Following this line of reasoning, Qfwfq comes to believe that a sign of his own making has instead created him. Once the sign exists outside or independently of the self, it can supposedly establish individual identity objectively, enabling him to then reverse the direction of his original concatenation of thoughts.

Now Qfwfq claims that because he writes, he exists (or so he would have us believe). When we look beyond this process of reification, we see that once the ego has created itself, it can project itself onto what is other through the act of writing, creating an external world in its own image. Thus, the constitution of subjectivity suppresses objectivity and establishes the subject-centric relativity on which Calvino grounds the cosmic ruminations of *Ti con zero*. Reality is established and defined by identity, which is the external manifestation of an internal consciousness. Interior reality creates and informs a world whose function is to assist the process of self-definition.[6]

Because of his fidelity to a unifying reality, which is consitituted in and around the organizing center of consciousness, plurality—of the other and of interpretation—represents an obstacle the Calvinian subject will not overcome. Rather than actively engage indeterminacy (in other words, exploit language's inability to reach the material referent, constantly deferring meaning between signifier and signified) he will, to use Ferretti's phrasing, "abdicate his right to narrate."

The conflict between monolithic consciousness and multiple interpretations is played out in "*Gli anni luce*." In Qfwfq's words, "it was important that the essential nature of all the things I did be put in relief, that the accent be placed in the right spot, that what should be noticed be duly noted and everything else ignored" (162). To accomplish this, he carries with him at all times signs that indicate which of his actions are significant and should be observed, and which disregarded, placing himself in a quintessentially Pirandellian situation.[7] To his mind, his intentions are univocal. But he also acknowledges that language is inadequate to unequivocally describe them (162) and that textualizations are all that remain of praxis. The origin of the text—Qfwfq's intentions—remains hidden from the viewer. Therefore, given the inadequacy of interpretation, perception and awareness by an-other are set aside in favor of what truly matters, internal consciousness. As arbitrary yet irrevocable interpretations of his actions proliferate, the creating consciousness is relieved to know that death will put *una pietra sopra* such "misunderstandings," precluding additions to and subtractions from the body of information furnished by a unitary, univocal existence. Death will give the final punctuation to identity (165).

Having thus achieved textual or biographical closure, the observer's gaze may revert to the past, to the origin of a nonanthropocentric world to be found in fossils and vestigial traces, the "now illegible language" (129), of the genetic text that survives in all species from eras that predate it ("*I dinosauri*").[8] The unifying consciousness and its construction of reality are part of an attempt by Calvino to plot a path back toward an all-authenticating foundational narrative. In "*Quanto scommettiamo,*" for example, the results of the events Qfwfq predicts, seen from our vantage point and that of the author Calvino, are already known. The abandonment of a future-oriented *progettualità* and the decision to embark on a trip backward in time are indicative of a desire to be reassured by the certainty of what is already known.

IV. Nonanthropocentrism

In a lengthy essay written in 1967, shortly after the death of his mentor Elio Vittorini ("*Vittorini: progettazione e letterature*" Ups 127–49), Calvino reflects on the former's influence on him while remembering how Vittorini saw the "beginning of Man as a qualitative leap" in the history of matter and the natural world. He then notes that unlike Vittorini, he aspired to "move toward a form of knowledge from which all anthropocentric residues are abolished, a form of knowledge in which the history of Man does not overextend its boundaries" (130–31). Calvino believed the internal dynamics of the human world reflected a larger process in which a finite number of atoms constantly rearranges itself. It was erroneous, in his opinion, to think that the problems afflicting humanity could be understood and dominated in isolation from a macroscopic system. He began to contemplate concentric totalities—human, natural, galactic—and seek out a universal system that could be reflected in narrative.

Contemporaneously, Calvino became increasingly interested in combinatoric literature advanced by Queneau and the OULIPO group.[9] Thus, his attention to contexts extraneous to humanity gave renewed vigor to a theory of narrative that fascinated him at least since his work on Italian fables: that of the combinatory potential of a finite number of minimal narrative units.[10]

The need to at least temporarily move away from a specifically anthropocentric vision is perhaps most clearly explained by Calvino in the essay "*Lo sguardo dell'archeologo*" (1972, Ups 263–66). Here he cited a crisis of civilization (as Calvino knew it) whose most salient symptoms were overpopulation, massive urbanization, and the end of Eurocentrism, and called for a rethinking of the human past and present from a supra- or nonhuman perspective. His long-range goal was the construction of a new master narrative that would "generalize and formalize the code of the primary operations of the human coordinator (*ordinatore*) and prior to that the code of the biological coordinator, and prior to that the mechanism of choices and elementary oppositions through which matter diversifies itself and communicates with itself" (265). The foundational narrative or basis for the self-authenticating truth to be gathered from all this would hopefully make clear to him "the norms which will make sense of chance, or the map of the prison which will allow us to reach a freedom, and then a general grammar of what exists" (Ups 265).

The overriding concern of the last two decades of Calvino's career is the search for a grounding narrative, a point of self-authentification. To that end, Calvino first sought out a human origin, and then a galactic one. To better understand and validate an anthropocentric vision, he went outside it to view it "objectively," from within the larger temporal and material context afforded by the cosmic totality. In other words, he hoped to uncover a cosmic metanarrative that would put into its proper perspective and help to explain the lesser, concentric, human totality. Although the importance of humanity is re-dimensioned in this scheme of things, it remains firmly at the center of investigation. In his *Lezione* on visibility, Calvino explained:

> One point to be cleared up about anthropomorphism in *Cosmicomics*: although I am interested in science because of its efforts to escape from anthropomorphic knowledge, I am nonetheless convinced that our imagination cannot be anything *but* anthropomorphic. This is the reason for my anthropomorphic treatment of a universe in which man has never existed. [90]

Contemplation of a cosmos that predates and will survive the collective human subject will cause Calvino to confront the Montalean void or the Borgesian "hide behind": nonbeing. As we will see, this question will be crucial to the last fifteen to twenty years of his life. It will culminate on the final page of *Palomar* when the autobiographical persona "imagines himself dead."

V. *Ti con zero*

In *Ti con zero* the short stories grouped under the heading "*Altri Qfwfq*" organize themselves around a series of hierarchical binary oppositions. Subtending "*La molle Luna*" is the juxtaposition of self and other; the earth is "diverse and superior" to its moon (16–17). Therefore the inhabitants of our planet take it onto themselves to eradicate, or at least conceal, all "alien and hostile effects" on the earth's essence unleashed by its natural satellite. The binary oppositions of "*Il sangue, il mare*" are those of self to other, life to death, interior to exterior. Qfwfq's copulation with Zylphia in "*Il sangue, il mare*" anticipates the discussion of procreation that gives cohesion to the "*Priscilla*" suite wherein the imbrications of self and other, inside and outside, and the compulsion to repeat or the death wish (159) inherent in the procreative act (the desire to project oneself into the future and attain immortality through a genetic heir) combine with the search for primordial origins ("the bloodthirsty instinct . . . that I carry with me—just as you do—in a polite and civil manner" [57]).

Other choices made from "among a limited number of possibilities" constitute the binary oppositions of evolutionary selection depicted in "*L'origine degli Uccelli*" (21). They allow Qfwfq to embrace a totality that simultaneously retraces the past to its origin and foresees all possible futures as they fan out before him:

> For a fraction of a second between the loss of all that I knew before and the acquisition of all that I would come to know later, I was able to embrace in a single thought the entire world as it was and the world as it might have been, and I understood that a single system contained everything." ["*L'origine degli Uccelli*" 31]

In this tale, the appearance of the ethnic other, the birds, introduces an element of disorder into an epistemological paradigm that previously had considered that particular life form discarded or superseded. That is to say, order, or normality, as defined by the bigoted paterfamilias U(h), is upset by the resurfacing of latent traces of the past. Relative order is quickly reestablished, however, when the world is divided into "monsters" and "nonmonsters" and the "monsters" are dutifully segregated to their own ghettoized space.

The perfect symmetry of "*I cristalli*" once again gives Qfwfq cause to ponder the relativity of the concepts of order and chaos as regards paths taken and not taken in the past. The *incipit* of this story describes an unexplored possibility. Had sufficient time been available when the earth cooled down from its original incandescent state, it might well have taken the shape of an enormous crystal, precluding life on the planet. The conflict in this story is between two contrasting conceptions of order: on the one hand there is Qfwfq's idea of an all-encompassing totality, a "single, gigantic crystal" (42). On the other hand we find Vhg's preference for the multiple, small totalities that constitute and continually reformulate the elements that comprise the whole: "the grid of atoms that continuously repeats itself" (41), and their "infinite separation and rejoining" (41).

"*Priscilla*" deals with traces latent within the genetic text and the manner in which it links us to the past to be uncovered through reverse translation: "the story of that which does not exist, and by not existing permits that which exists to exist" (*la storia di ciò che non esiste e non esistendo fa sí che ciò che esiste esista* [92]). It also explores further the hypostatization of time and space by consciousness. The observing subject ("happy . . . to mark with my presence the passage of time. . . . But please keep in mind that my being there also meant existing in space" [69–70]) can project external points of orientation after constructing an identity that enables him to distinguish himself from what is other.

Once again, Qfwfq thinks and therefore the world exists. At the same time, he notices that space and time are "a potential projection of myself from which, however, I was absent and therefore a void that was in sum the world and the future but I did not know it yet" (70). The subject exists by dint of its projection of interior reality onto an exterior world whose function is to document the subject's self-expression:

> When the world does not exist or you don't know that it exists, you feel the urge to do something, anything, anything at all. But when you cannot do anything because there is no external world, the only thing you can do—because of the limited means at your disposal—is that special sort of doing that we call self-expression. [74-75]

The question of identity is raised once more in "*Meiosi*," this time among more developed species, along with the theme of the forking paths. Qfwfq would like to know if identity is defined by a system of differences and similarities—by contrasting the self to what it is not—or if identity is intrinsic and irrevocably determined by the genetic code:

> That which each of us truly is and has is the past; all that we are and have is the catalog of possibilities that have not failed to be realized, the experiences that can be repeated. The present does not exist, we proceed blindly toward the beyond and the after, developing a program that has been established with materials we do not create but recycle. We do not move toward a future, nothing waits for us, we are merely part of a memory that foresees nothing but the memory of itself. [87–88]

Qfwfq creates and then inhabits a time-space totality that contains all potentialities. The limits of time and space coincide with Qfwfq's awareness of them; he knows "neither a before nor an after" and space extends only to the bounds of perception. In "*Mitosi*," for example, he experiences a Kunderian "lightness of being," where the weight of a determining history is reduced to that of the unrealized potentialities latent within the present. Everything we have been, are, and may become is contained in the original one-cell organism that is Qfwfq: "what matters is the moment in which you break away from yourself and feel in a flash the union of past and future" (81).

VI. "Deductive Tales"[11]

The concluding section of *Ti con zero* also deals with the relativity of time and space. The stories grouped together here provide a valuable point of reference for retracing the final two decades of Calvino's career. Within this suite, the narrative "*Il conte di Montecristo*" represents, in Calvino's opinion, one of his "points of arrival" (Camon 187). To underscore the importance of the "Deductive Tales," after they first appeared *Ti con zero*, Calvino republished them as a unit at the conclusion of both *Cosmicomiche vecchie e nuove* and *La memoria del mondo*. In these four brief narratives the centrality of the subject who informs external reality by projection is reaffirmed. In the eponymous short story and in "*L'inseguimento*" Qfwfq rejects the concept of objective time (118) and space: "no space," he claims, "exists independently of the bodies that occupy it" (132).

In the "Deductive Tales" Calvino's investment in the subject is complete; all action takes place within the mind of the persona. In "*Il guidatore notturno*" the immanent narrator is sealed in his car, completely removed from human consortium, immersed in a darkness punctuated only by the occasional headlights of other automobiles:

> If tonight I am willing to reflect on it, it is because now the external possibilities of distraction diminish and the internal ones have taken over; my thoughts run away from me in their own circuit of alternatives and doubts that I am unable to defuse. [141]

Because of the complete introversion of the subject, objective time and space are obliterated ("I feel as if I've lost the sense of space and of time" [142]) and, with them, comunication: "speeding down the highway is the only possibility left to her and me to express what we need to say to each other, but we can not begin to communicate as long as we are speeding in opposite directions" (144).

Because of its *dei ex machina* "*L'inseguimento*" is probably the least artistically successful of the stories. It finds Qfwfq at the outset in "pseudo-space." It is "pseudo" because Qfwfq does not construct it intellectually. Instead his range of maneuver is objectively limited by a traffic jam. Once this limitation on the individual's freedom to think his environment is overcome (that is to say, as soon as space becomes once again a purely intellectual construct uninfluenced by external factors), Qfwfq cannot only dominate it, but he can theoretically abolish it (132) and he can contemplate a space that is both relative to him and of his own creation. The distance Qfwfq perceives between himself and his would-be assassin becomes the only real space. It gives shape, in Qfwfq's mind, to a "general system." This "general system," once created, envelopes Qfwfq and takes him "prisoner" (137): the intellect is bound or predetermined by its own constructs.

In "*Ti con zero*" Qfwfq once again thinks his environment, and tries to create through deduction a "general system" that predetermines and limits the possibilities of agency. If time's grand scheme is a finite system that follows a pattern of cyclical self-repetition, he reasons, "of what use is carrying on . . . sooner or later we have to return to where we are now" (110). However, he continues, perhaps time is a combinatoric totality, centered in the present, composed of an infinite number of possibilities:

> If an infinite number of possible futures fan out from this specific point in time, then those same lines must begin somewhere in the past where they too form a cone of infinite possibilities. [113]

At the tale's end, the contradiction remains unresolved: time may follow a linear path, or the present, "*ti con zero*," may fall at the intersection of an infinite number of virtual pasts and futures. Because of this, he is unable to ascertain the correct posture to assume: "If I want to remain frozen in time, I must flow with time; if I want to be objective, I must remain subjective" (118).

The condition of the self-imposed intellectual prison is addressed again in "*Il conte di Montecristo*." The narrating persona, Edmond Dantès, is physically and mentally separated from the world and outside time. His only space for maneuver is within the mind. He would measure time in spatial terms, but, as he puts it, "at most, I can fix in time a succession of points that have no spatial counterparts" (152). In contradistinction, the Abbot Faria hopes to retrace through space the historical time of his imprisonment back to the moment of his incarceration. He believes that if he can do this, he can escape from the Isle of If (158).

Dantès knows that Faria's efforts are destined to fail, but considers the abbot a "necessary complement" for his own elucubrations (154). He also knows that escape from or even the transformation of a prison whose substance is time is inconceivable because it continuously "grows around us, and the longer we remain closed within it, the more we are distanced from the outside" (158). Nonetheless, he believes he can transcend the *condition* of prisoner: unlike Faria who would write a linear narrative or causal history of the past, Dantès imagines a "general system" or combinatoric totality:

> The concentric fortress If-Montecristo-Dumas's writing desk holds us prisoner along with the treasure, the hypernovel *Montecristo* with its finite number—there are billions and billions of combinations, mind you—of variants. Faria would really like to find a single page or solution among them, and is fully confident he will. I prefer to watch the pile of discarded pages of the jettisoned narrative solutions grow. A cluster of heaps have already risen up and now form a great wall. [163]

Faria's "page among the many" aims at a narrative diegesis with a beginning and an end. Dantès's "discarded pages constitute an all-inclusive *combinatoire*, or "library of Babel," within which the metafictional recycling of the narrative materials of the past can take place.

This particular "deductive tale" constitutes a significant point of arrival in Calvino's intellectual biography. It marks the rise of a poetics grounded in combinatorics and the concurrent demise of deductive reasoning as an investigative tool. From this point forward no "general system" will predetermine the articulation of any combinatoric totality. Instead, the particular will be the point of departure for the construction of the totality through inductive thought.

VII. *La memoria del mondo* and *Cosmicomiche vecchie e nuove*

Consideration of the final collection of Qfwfq tales, *Cosmicomiche vecchie e nuove* (significantly the last volume of fiction published by Calvino before his death), shows that two stories, "*Le conchiglie e il tempo*" and "*La memoria del mondo*," appear exclusively in *La memoria del mondo*. Two others—"*Il niente e il poco*" and "*L'implosione*"—appear for the first time in *Cosmicomiche vecchie e nuove*. The latter volume reconfigures all the cosmicomic tales except "*Le conchiglie e il tempo*" and "*La memoria del mondo*," suggesting that they are indicative of a cognitive strategy explored and subsequently abandoned. At the same time, the inclusion in *Cosmicomiche vecchie e nuove* of new tales of contemporaneous gestation as the pieces collected in *Palomar* and *Collezione di sabbia* can be used to help put in relief the direction Calvino's work was taking in the years immediately preceding his death.

Of the eight new cosmicomic tales that appear in *La memoria del mondo*, six are republished in *Cosmicomiche vecchie e nuove*. The two that are discarded will be considered presently as examples of a tack abandoned by Calvino in favor of the phenomenological defamiliarization that characterizes the prose of his final years. The other six stories appear in pairs in the first three sections of *La memoria del mondo*. Two are about the moon, two are about the earth, and two are about the sun. The new earth and sun tales (*"Il cielo di pietra," "I meteoriti," "Fino a che dura il Sole,"* and *"Tempesta solare"*) confront the reader with binary oppositions, fundamental choices that determined the subsequent development of the cosmos and of life on earth. *"Il cielo di pietra"* contrasts what is inside and outside the earth's crust to cast in relief a path not taken, what for us will always be "elsewhere and otherwise" (61). In a similar fashion, Rah, in *"Tempesta solare"* confronts the reader with "a different way of being" from our own. *"I meteoriti"* and *"Fino a che dura il Sole"* juxtapose visions of order and disorder. *"I meteoriti"* leads the reader to ask, what exactly *is* the natural order of things? The conflict of order and disorder forces the immanent narrator to choose between interior calm coupled with exterior disorder or its opposite, exterior order coupled with interior disquietude. This "continuous tumult" (71) finally produces a "general disorder you had to believe was the natural order of things" (71). In *"fino a che dura il Sole"* Colonel Eggg's love of "contemplating the ordered and regular traffic of the universe" (139) is continually disturbed by his wife's irrepressible tendency to introduce elements of chaos into their lives.

The two new stories in the section on the moon, *"Le figlie della Luna"* and *"La Luna come un fungo,"* place humanity at a juncture of forking paths or evolutionary crossroads. *"Le figlie della Luna"* allegorically shows society at the brink of self-destruction. The dying moon, symbol of a natural environment violated by a rapid and unplanned industrialization run amock, falls from the sky over Manhattan—capital, to paraphrase Benjamin, of the twentieth century. The moon, in *"La Luna come un fungo"*—a tale that depicts the alteration of the course of evolution on the earth caused by the birth of the moon—is "the negation of the [human] world" (120) and Bm Bn is evil incarnate. The story reads in fact like a preanthropomorphic morality play. It registers the struggle between two metaphysical traits, good (Qfwfq) and evil (Bm Bn). This conflict is in part catalyzed and ultimately presided over by the apolitical Inspector (the scientist whose pure research willfully ignores the practical consequences of his discoveries) and a "gentile and remissive young woman" (121). Ultimately, Bm Bn uses neutral or disinterested science to exploit natural resources and subjugate his fellows.[12]

La memoria del mondo is the final configuration given the tales in the late 1960s. The eponymous tale is grouped significantly in the concluding cluster of "deductive tales" that deal with the relativity of time and space, temporarily taking the place within the suite of "*Ti con zero*" (which will reappear in *Cosmicomiche vecchie e nuove*). Its companions in this section are "*L'inseguimento*," "*Il guidatore notturno*" and "*Il conte di Montecristo*," stories whose importance has already been underscored. The other tale that appears exclusively in *La memoria del mondo*, "*Le conchiglie e il tempo*," immediately precedes the eponymous narrative (it comes at the end of a section dedicated to evolution) and deals with the question of a historical continuum. The theme of "La memoria del mondo" is the textualization of lived praxis and its deliberate falsification.

What must be asked of these tales, particularly when read in light of the two that will appear for the first time in *Cosmicomiche vecchie e nuove*, is whether or not they represent elements of continuity or discontinuity in Calvino's *ouevre*, or at least a shift in emphasis away from the self-sufficient individual consciousness of the three volumes of cosmicomic tales published in the 1960s.

In "*Le conchiglie e il tempo*" Qfwfq, like Edmond Dantès, is prisoner of an "interminable present," condemned to live "minute by minute" outside the flow of history. Yet in spite of this, or because of this, he claims to be the arteficer of time: "if it were not for me, time would not exist" (Mm 161). After the fashion of "*La spirale*," here the problem of constructing the concept of time is connected to the creation of a shell. The question centers on how to "establish a direction and a norm" while surrounded by the undifferentiated natural cycles of days and nights, the sun and moon, the waves, tides and seasons (161, 162).

Qfwfq's proposal is to make "signs in time" (162) by distinguishing the subjective time of consciousness from the flow of chronological time (162). His exterior sign is a shell, which once again constitutes an external manifestation of an interiority: "what I wanted to build for myself, in short, was a time that was exclusively mine, regulated only by me, refractory" (162). He sets out believing that one subjective representation can embrace all existence, but comes to understand that no one can alone construct an "endless spiral" (162). Objective time is the sum of the myriad individual consciousnesses of it, a totality of multiplicities: "using our interrupted spirals you have put together a continuous spiral that you call history" (164).[13] It exists because it is preserved in textual traces (in this instance the shells) which posterity (re)interprets:

> I might add that part of the credit should go to you, you knew how to read what was written between the lines, (you see, here I go again, using your metaphor, writing, you can't get away from it, it just goes to show we are playing on your home court, not mine), you succeeded in making something out of our mixed alphabet and of piecing together what we scattered over silence. You put together a coherent, cogent discourse *all about yourselves*. [163-64]

In *Cosmicomiche vecchie e nuove* two new tales are added to those published at least sixteen years earlier. What becomes even more evident when we contrast the two tales just described and the two new stories included in *Cosmicomiche vecchie e nuove* is the shift from an Idealistic, Crocean view of the subject to a phenomenological one. A unifying view of the universe centered in the individual is common to both perspectives. For Qfwfq, *vecchio* and *nuovo*, the universe and the subject's perspective of it, are synonymous. However, the conflict of nothingness, being and nonbeing that subtends the stories new to *Cosmicomiche vecchie e nuove*—"*Il niente e il poco*" and "*L'implosione*"—is also at the core of *Palomar*.

For the old, Crocean Qfwfq, time exists only in the subject's consciousness. For the new Qfwfq, time enjoys an existence autonomous of consciousness, in the nothingness that precedes it and in the nonbeing (the Montalean void) to follow. Nothingness, for Qfwfq is "a place where I could have existed" ([*dove avrei potuto essere*] "*Il niente e il poco*" Cvn 209), a totality of potentialities where everything and nothing exist side by side:

> It is a sort of existence where if you're there, you're there, and if you're not, you're not, and if you're not, you can begin to count on being there, and then wait and see what happens. This was certainly a big deal for us, because only if you begin to exist virtually, to fluctuate in a field of probability, to give and take charges of hypothetical energy can you hope to one day exist in fact, in other words to bend around yourself your own small share of space-time. [209–10]

Qfwfq acknowledges that nothingness, or *il nulla di prima* (210), existed prior to his cognizance of it, when he was merely a potentiality within nothingness. The state of being that followed was a rush to "embrace the totality" (210), to extend, that is, oneself forward in space and time (211). It is subtended by a death wish, a compulsion to repeat, to return to the equilibrium of nonbeing:

> I don't know if I knew it then or if I learned only now that behind this exaltation was an insecurity, a mania to erase even the shade of our collective origins. Because notwithstanding the certainty that everything was part of our natural environment, it was also true that we had come up from nothing, that we had brought ourselves up from absolute propertylessness, that only a slim thread of space-

> time separated us from our previous condition, when we were without substance, magnitude, and endurance. We were filled with rapid but sharp feelings of precariousness. It was as if this totality was trying to give itself a shape in order to hide its own innate fragility and the nothingness to which we could all return just as quickly as we transformed out of it. [211]

Being is a period that falls between that of existence as potentiality (nothingness) and the inevitable return to nonbeing. Nothingness comes to be seen as an almost Edenic state forever lost, a finite, "invincible absolute," "the only authentic totality possible" (214). Finally Qfwfq understands that life is not a *tutto*—as was the *niente* that preceded it—but a *poco*. Being is existence as a determinate amalgam of atoms, the realization of one of the potential totalities contained in nothingness, the intermediate stage between nothingness and nonbeing.

"*L'implosione*" depicts the inverse of the process of expansion described in "*Il niente e il poco.*" Paraphrasing Hamlet, Qfwfq perorates on the existential question that subtends much of what Calvino writes during the final years of his life. As Qfwfq puts it, "to explode or implode, that is the question" (217): "*Io implodo*," he proclaims (218). [. . .] That is to say, he moves away from the determinate toward the infinite potentialities of nothingness. As he does, a second explosion, the *deflagrazione generale* (218) of nuclear annihilation, echoes the original, that of the Big Bang that gave birth to the cosmos, prefiguring the compression of organic being in a black hole wherein the cycle will begin afresh when the contents of that vortex are "reshuffled," as it were, and nonbeing ebbs into nothingness.

After doubling the arrow of time (that is, reversing time's exclusively forward direction), an imploding Qfwfq contemplates saving or redeeming his exploding counterpart. However, the reversibility of time is not the issue. Qfwfq's only concern is his discovery of the vanification of action by the instinctive compulsion to return to an inanimate state:

> Every journey in time, forward and backward, heads toward disaster; the intersection of these journeys does not form an ordered network but an entanglement. [220-21]

The labyrinth in which this new Qfwfq must live offers no hope of transcendence. Moreover, while Dantès's metafictional, self-authenticating existence equated writing and being, this Qfwfq recognizes phenomena that exist independently of the writing subject. In fact, in "*Il niente e il poco*" we see that the opposition of implosion and explosion is indeed an interrogation into the nature of being and nonbeing. The nothing evoked in the title, the "only authentic totality possible" (214), is a totality-potentiality in which all other possible totalities are contained, both what exists (has existed, will exist) and the myriad paths not taken that will never enter into being. Qfwfq finally comes to the conclusion:

> All that is contained in space and time is insignificant (*il poco*). Begotten from nothingness, the little that exists could also not exist, or it could exist in an even more meager form, more emaciated and perishable. If we prefer to not speak about this, it is because we can only say, "poor delicate universe, child of nothingness, in all that we are and do we resemble you." [Cvn 215]

3 Interlude: Late Modernist Metafiction. The Example of John Barth

I. Realism, Modernism, Postmodernism

In the essay "Literature of Replenishment," John Barth held up two novels by Calvino as "exemplary postmodernist" writings (*The Friday Book* 204).[1] Calvino, too, on at least one occasion, spoke of his reciprocal interest in Barth's work and of their friendship (*Mal d'America* 161). Beyond such personal bonds, the work of the two writers both emphasize the use of combinatoric, or better, metafictional rearranging of timeless narrative archetypes, recuperated from within a Borgesian "library of Babel." Like Calvino, Barth has described the act of writing as one in which received works are "reorchestrat[ed] to present purpose." Just as Calvino brings together in his prose nonharmonious harmonies, in "How to Make a Universe" Barth evokes a "preestablished harmony" (*The Friday Book* 19)—very similar to the atemporal, basic narrative units Calvino identifies and utilizes in *Il castello dei destini incrociati*—he then discombobulates and reconfigures to make his own narrative universe.

In this chapter I will argue that the late modernisms of Barth and Calvino do not cause the erasure, or what Roland Barthes called the death, of the author. Neither Calvino's nor Barth's author abdicates responsibility for the text. Instead the radical subjectivity of the metafictionist "culminates," to borrow Barth's phrasing, "not merely in a theophany but in an apotheosis" (*The Friday Book* 75): the elevation of the writer to the godlike status of unifying textual consciousness. In Barth's writings this takes shape through two interwoven processes: the first is the use of the frametale devise; the other is the metafictional recuperation of basic, archetypal elements of plot.

Barth writes in extraliterary contexts of the frametale strategy as a means of enveloping lived reality within everlarger retellings until life is overtaken and fictionalized. In "The Self in Fiction," he claims that the defining characteristic of postmodern prose is the heightened self-consciousness of the author (*The Friday Book* 209). In order to produce a text, the author must first create a narrating persona, which is an extension of the author's personality. Thus, the act of producing a text "fictionalizes" the author's life. The "self-conscious" author, having "perpetrated" the first fiction, the creation of a narrating persona, uses the persona to "frame" or "surround" the narrative. Readers then "frame" text and author by "reading/narrating" the work. Hence, the inherent fictionality of the author's—and by extension everyone else's—life.

Just as the immanent narrator and the fiction are framed by the author who creates them, when text and author become the object of reading-narration, they too are "framed" and "fictionalized" by the reader, effecting what for Barth is the equation of life and fiction: life is fiction, fiction is life.

Barth's "self-conscious" writer is also keenly aware of the literary tradition and of the need to "replenish" both it and and him/herself by recycling elements of plot common to all narratives. In so doing, the metafictionist attains the timeless universality of the Ur-myth of "exhaustion and replenishment/resurrection." To explain, Barth's persona in *Once Upon a Time* follows the paradigmatic voyage of the wandering hero (309ff.). His prospected "kenosis" or "replenishment" (13–14) collimates with both the autotelic (re)searching and (re)writing of the past and with the act of writing about writing in the present (54, 57). What is specific to the immanent narrator is then transcended by a "unitive experience" (316) wherein the reader, whose life experiences loosely parallel those recounted, identifies with the narrator.

Therefore, the loosely autobiographical persona of *Once Upon a Time* feels justified in positing his own condition as microcosm: his here and now "*is* the universe" (58). The narrative voice, all the more typical because he—like the rest of us, to borrow Barth's phrasing, "lowercase" heroes (as opposed to the "uppercase derring-doers of the Ur-myth—Theseus, Perseus, Oedipus, Odysseus, Aeneas, Watu Gunung, Siegfried, Dante's Dante" [324])—understands there is no short cut through the labyrinth. The narrative voice triumphs when he persists in writing (or "penning," which for the persona "comes as naturally as breathing" [28]). With pen ("literal link" between mind, body, and page [26]) in hand, and ear stopples in place (28), he detaches himself from his surroundings and meets his self-imposed goal, that of speaking "eloquently and memorably to our human hearts and conditions" (*The Friday Book* 67). Life is (re)lived on sheets of paper fecundated by pens. It is narrated, fictionalized, and ultimately transcended when we understand that to live is to write, and that writing is synonymous with the replenishment of the all-encompassing grand narrative of literature.

Federman has described metafiction as a literature that sets social commitment aside in order to "concern itself with itself, with literature, with the crisis of literature, with the crisis of language" and to "comunicate with the crisis of knowledge, and not with social and political problems" (*Critifiction* 5). Because of this retreat from the world, esthetic and stylistic concerns predominate in metafiction.[2] After discounting and divorcing itself from contemporary society, self-reflexive metafiction claims to supplant the world outside its self-demarcated parameters. Therefore, late modernist metafiction does not seek mimetically to reflect reality, but further narrows the scope of self-conscious, high modernist prose by reducing the thinking *I* of the latter to its own writing/reading *I*.

High modernist narratives, because of their lost faith in a shared objective reality, depict introverted, first-person microcosms. In so doing, they distinguish themselves from classic realist fiction, which was grounded in an empirical conception of typical reality and utilized an omniscient, third-person perspective as its center of gravity (even though multiple centers of consciousness can be reflected omnisciently in a realist narrative). However, even though the first-person subjectivity of modernist prose signaled a break with the third-person objectivity of nineteenth-century realism, both realist and modernist fictions utilized a unifying perspective centered in the narrating consciousness. This is also the case with the ultraindividualistic self-reflexive metafiction.

Indeed, what differentiates high from late literary modernism is the latter's further retreat inward from the objectifiable world and its radical, self-reflexive turn into literature and the act of writing. The "self-consciousness, self-knowledge, and self-transcendence" of late modernist metafiction (*Once Upon a Time* 118) circumscribe it within Frye's grand narrative of literature, a conceptual framework or coordinating principle that can be applied to the internal functioning of literature, while hermetically sealing literature off from its social humus.

II. The "Death" or Abdication of the Author

According to Federman, there is "too much to know and comprehend" and so the contemporary writer can neither represent the world nor, for that matter, completely express his/her inner self. Since reality cannot be embraced in its entirety, authors can "legitimately" do no more than write about their own experiences. What replaces knowledge of the world, in Federman's words, is the self-reflective act "of searching (researching even) within the fiction itself for the implications of what it means to write fiction" (*Critifiction* 10). Unable to know the world, the author forfeits the right to impose meaning on the text. The reader, "no longer manipulated by an authorial point of view," as Federman wrote in an earlier essay, "will be the one who extracts, invents, creates a meaning and an order for the people in the fiction" ("Surfiction" 14). When the "dead" author cedes or loses the right to impose meaning, the center of gravity supposedly shifts from the producer to the consumer(s) of the text. However, the transferral of responsibility to multiple readers does not forestall the privileging of any one reading (this is particularly the case with Umberto Eco, as we shall see in the Afterword).

In metafiction the unifying consciousness of the writer reaffirms itself. Thus, the unifying center of narrative gravity or authorial consciousness of nineteenth-century realism and the high modernism of the first half of this century is also common to late modernist metafiction. Their unifying perspective differentiates them from oppositional postmodernisms characterized by their use of heterotelic first-person narratives. Oppositional postmodernisms, as we shall see in chapter six, do not underwrite the late modernist "death of the author," wherein the decentering process hinges on the purported abdication of the author's right to narrate and consequent transferral of responsibility for the creation of the text to the reader. Contestatory postmodern narratives recognize equally valid and diverse points of view and refute linear, univocal renderings of the past.

The metafictionist questioning of the author's right to impose meaning or narrate comes in response to the realist's certainty about literature's " 'right to exist' in an objective world" (Smart 8) and after almost a century of modernist grappling with relativity. The late modernist understands that the literary representation of an indeterminate reality must somehow be legitimized. Also, as Smart reminds us, for the metafictionist the only reality the writer controls is what s/he writes. Therefore metafiction, in order to validate itself, turns inward, away from its indeterminate surroundings and toward what it can dominate—self-consciousness—thereby transforming the *process* of writing into the *subject* of writing. Then, by coopting the reader and requiring the reader to rewrite the text, metafiction coaxes the reader into identifying with the narrating consciousness, ostensibly to complete the process of writing, but in truth to witness the self-legitimation and authentication of the narrative. In Smart's words, "unlike the conventional 'totalizing' novel," the autobiographical or metafictional novel, "mirrors a reality constructed from the author's personal experience within the text, and not from an external reality which 'ought' to reflect the reader's own." When reality is circumscribed within the parameters of the text, "the two composing *processes* (reading and writing) are identical" (11). Corroboration by the reader of the writer's reality becomes unnecessary because the written page authenticates itself by echoing canonical traces of the literary tradition within the writing consciousness. Therefore, prior to and precluding the reader's identification with the writing consciousness and the opening of the floodgates of the free play of multiple interpretation, the reader is subsumed within the text and the author's capacity to predetermine subsequent readings is reaffirmed.

Edwards's deconstructionist reading of Barth and Calvino claims that the two writers' solicitation of reader participation in the creation of meaning privileges all readings. However, the "deprivileging" of an author's "definitive reading" is at best questionable when applied to metafiction, wherein the author constitutes the text's primary reader. The metafictional text is not an absence—*there* where writer and reader, the subject and the object of linguistic desire, are *not* (Barthes)—because the metafictional text is first and foremost a presence, there where both subject (author) and object of desire (primary, or privileged reader) *are*. In metafiction the text is primarily a use value or interior monologue. Only later and incidentally does it transform into a dialogic means of linguistic exchange. In *Once Upon a Time* what is external to imagination is disregarded: the writing process is significantly defined as a "*self-organized* criticality" (20, my emphasis). Through "coaxial esemplasy" (as Barth defines it, "the ongoing, reciprocal shaping of our story [in this case a story of our life] by our imagination, and of our imagination by our story thus far" [20]) existence is circumscribed by the authorial consciousness of it and its reflection on the page.

Calvino has stated that by attempting to "run away from the author," through the multiplication of the writing *I* in *Se una notte un viaggiatore*, he was, in point of fact, endeavoring to "reach the anonymous *I* of writing" ("Italo Calvino: Videotheque"). By his own account, Calvino's flight from the author consisted of substituting the writer with a reader (*Lettore*), whose function, in Calvino's plan, was to underscore the *Lettrice*'s need of a definitive author of the stories she would passively read. Paradoxically, for Calvino the abolition of the author gives proof of the author's existence: it "demonstrates," in the novelist's own words, "*that one cannot make do without the author*" ("Italo Calvino: Videotheque").

In fact, as Motte has indicated, the "interactive," exaggerated, "unavoidably apparent structure" of another novel that is often held up as a paradigmatic "postmodern" novel, *Il castello dei destini incrociati*, seems to openly solicit the reader's participation, attenuating traditional narrative authority. However, in effect, the author's "right to narrate" is reaffirmed when the reader's ability to critically interpret the text is preempted and absorbed by the writing consciousness. The answer to the question, Who writes the text?, as is the case with Barth's *Once Upon a Time*, is the author. As Motte writes:

> If the narrator seems to offer readers a share in his activity, he nonetheless plays another significant game in his attempts to seduce them. For the narrator of *The Castle of Crossed Destinies* is clearly first and foremost a *reader* himself. That is, his reading of the cards, of the unvoiced tales presented by the other characters, is logically prior to his narration. Reader as narrator, narrator as reader: the apparent subversion of the traditional separation of labor in literature is located precisely on the highest level of the game. [127]

In other words, there is no egalitarian democracy of "isomorphic" readings. The author is the privileged reader.

Linda Hutcheon has argued that all texts create a "fictional universe" that is not empirically perceived but imagined and actualized by a reader ("Metafictional Implications"). If this is the case, the world imagined by the *privileged* reader (the author) becomes more real than life itself, real to the second power, because relived. When circumscribed within the "personal universe" (*Once Upon a Time* 58) of a narrator who has foresworn dialogic authentication or objectification, relived experience validates itself through sheer redundancy. To use Barth's own words, the metafictionist "learn[s] by going where [he's already] been" (393). Indeed, in order to transform experience into writing, the metafictionist must conflate perceived and apperceived reality. Apperceived (or relived) reality "falsifies" or "fictionalizes" life by cognitively restructuring and textualizing it.

Transcribers of their own lives, such as Svevo's Zeno and Vecchione and Barth's metafictional narrators, find themselves, to use Hutcheon's term, in a "Pirandellian relativity paradox" when they confuse lived, perceived, empirical reality and what is subsequently apperceived, textualized, and read-imagined-actualized. They then allow the latter to supplant the former because imagined-actualized reality not only "mimes" the cognitive process, but, because of its linguistic coherency, apperception "is the means to the only lucidity one can ever know" ("Metafictional Implications" 6). Indeed, in Pirandello and Svevo, the narrating personae are more concerned with thinking and writing about life than they are with experiencing it.

Barth's heroes go one step further; they bypass the introspection of these high modernist forebears and write only about writing. The conflict however, for both high and late modernists, is resolved within the unifying perspective of the author. As Barth stresses in *Once Upon a Time*, the hero of his "memoir in a novel" ("Program Note") is able to make his way through life's maze, because "*the sentences get written*" (396). Implicit here is the discounting of the work or praxis of writing and the privileging of its traces—the words and sentences that remain on the page, textualized life, which become tantamount to life itself, the word made flesh.

III. The Frametale

Self-reflexive metafiction claims to subsume the "dead" writer within the text and supplant the world: reality is fictitious and fiction is real. It does not pretend to serve as means of exchange between the writer and society. Despite such claims, human praxis is not overtaken by metafiction. Rather the life that is "lived" on the printed page is supplanted when the writer identifies with the act of writing and hermetically withdraws from the world outside the text. Barth and Federman do well to claim that life is overtaken by fiction. However, this is the case only when life is defined not as lived experience, but as the subsequent textualization of that experience. In Federman's

might infuse "that literary past with new meaning." Although the writer can no longer be "original," Menard prompted Barth to realize that ageless stories, or myths, can always be recycled and told in new ways. Quoting one of Borges's editors, Barth wrote: "all writers are more or less faithful amanuenses of the spirit, translators and annotators of pre-existing archetypes"—timeless archetypes, it should be parenthetically added, that coincide with the "constitutive principles of story-telling" evoked by Northrop Frye. Barth found Borges's "library of Babel" "particularly pertinent" to the question of the exhaustion and replenishment of literature because the library combinatorically houses all possibilities of narrative choice. Lost within the totality of the library, the body of the metafictionist's work, a smaller totality, is unified by its author's perspective.

In "Literature of Replenishment" (1980) Barth took pains to clarify this earlier essay and explained that, through the conscious recuperation of certain aspects of realist narration, the style of writing he was beginning to call "postmodernist" was able to go beyond the "subjective distortion" (199) characteristic of modernism, synthesize the "exhausted" narrative strategies of realism and high modernism, and—by contemporaneously recycling the mythic narratives addressed in "Literature of Exhaustion"—"replenish" literature. For Barth, as for Pirandello, the unifying consciousness of the author provides the fictive universe of his/her own creation with its lost oneness.

Significantly, in "Literature of Replenishment" one of Barth's citations of Borges is highly reminiscent of the Sicilian playwright. Barth wrote:

> In one piece [Borges] imagines [Shakespeare] on his deathbed asking God to permit him to be one and himself, having been everyone and no one; God replies from the whirlwind that He is no one either: He has dreamed the world like Shakespeare, and including Shakespeare. [74].

The author, like God, is no one and one hundred thousand, yet both achieve oneness through their creation.

In contradistinction to Pirandello's explicit—and Barth's implicit—attempts to reconstitute a monolithic *I*, Tabucchi has spoken of the alloglossia that informs his *Requiem*. In a paper read at a conference on translation, he concluded that writing in a language other than one's own has a therapeutic value that serves not to reconcile two aspects of a personality, but to help the *I* accept the two in their diversity ("Some Reflections on Translation").

Tabucchi goes on to affirm that the search for "nobody" in his novel *Notturno indiano* (and we can say the same for *Il filo dell'orizzonte*) is a search for the self. As is the case with Pirandello, *I* equals nobody for Tabucchi also, because both writers acknowledge the indeterminacy of identity. However, Tabucchi accepts the irreconcilable plurality of diversities within (and without) the relativistic point of reference that is the conscious ego. Pirandello, on the other hand, would reconstitute the physical, anagraphic, and, most important, psychic integrity of what is perceived in one hundred thousand different ways by as many others as it happens to encounter.

The polycentric perspective of postmodern narratives, as we shall see in a subsequent chapter, calls to task received modernist notions of subjectivity. The radical subjectivity of Barth's late modernist metafiction, on the other hand, does not challenge any received cognitive norms so much as it reaffirms the unity of the narrating consciousness through the investiture of the author as first reader and the surreptitious refusal of dialogic interaction with what is outside the text.

The eschatological trope of death and resurrection implicit in the metafictional enterprise of "replenishing" an "exhausted" literary tradition is subtley recuperated in *Once Upon a Time*, a work Barth could have easily titled, *pace* Whitman, "Song of Myself" (see 163, 386). The immanent narrator of this text relives the "'Ur-myth' [or] archetypal pattern of wandering-hero myths." He embarks on a voyage, in this case a "typical midlife process" (8), of personal "replenishment" to be realized in the yet-to-be-written/lived "Act Three." In *Once Upon a Time* Barth doubles the I of narration into "writer and penman" (21), narrating I (writer) and Barth himself (penman and word-processing reader-correcter of the narrative, first reader and annotator of the text; most certainly *not* the "general reader" [88], nor the "particular reader" [88] nor the "dedicatee" of the work).

The splitting of the authorial consciousness, as we have seen, does not undermine the narrator's authority but in fact reaffirms it. Moreover, the narrating *I* is itself divided into the several "internalized" (300, 312) monologic counterparts, the alter egos and "counterselves" who "guide" him through the text, creating a polyphonic effect that in truth is composed of a single voice. The reunion of the "penman" and the immanent narrator—and reestablishment of the unified consciousness—is effected in the *temps retrouvé* of the narration when absence (memory) becomes presence (text) and life transpires on the point of a pen. Barth's immanent narrator must lose his pen, or "identity-token" and totem of his written/lived existence in time, in the "funhouse of fiction" so that the Ur-mythical journey may begin (315):

> Time's arrow on the butted cap point pointward, to where the ongoing present's nib resistlessly pasts the future, elucidating all three. [364]

Once the pen has been dropped overboard, the "wandering hero" may rethink his life and begin to approach an answer to Everyman's "first and final narrative question": "Who am I?" (319). The autotelic journey never exceeds the confines of the unifying consciousness of the narrator because "the medium [of writing] is the message" (54). The answer to the written writer's "ultimate question" is I am what I write, or better, I write, therefore I am.

tive human behavior. Thus, the pessimistic ending of "*La città e i morti*" can be read in counterpoint to the more optimistic panorama of Andria, which depicts a productive understanding of the relationship between microcosm and cosmos. By the same token, the extremely bleak view of the future presented in "*Le città continue*" can be juxtaposed to the ensuing, ambivalent, final rubic, "*Le città nascoste*." What is "continuous" in Polo's cities is the pollution, social homologation, overpopulation, and urban sprawl of industrialized society. "*Le città nascoste*" on the other hand are visions of contemporary society at a juncture of forking paths, a potentially "happy city, unaware of its own existence" contained *in nuce* within the present-day "unhappy city" (155).

The pendant of Berenice, a city in which history follows a cyclical pattern of alternating periods of justice and injustice, is found in the framing tale of Polo and Kan. Since the quality and nature of the bonds between humans give contemporary cities their shape (154), we may speculate with Polo on what is to come: all will be contingent on the further refinement or degradation of human relations (160). However, the cyclical depiction of history (just as good contains the seed of evil, evil incubates good [166]) adds to the overall pessimism by underscoring the futility of human agency. As the work ends, the extermination of the natural world and the uncontested predominance of humanity over all other life forms on the planet leave the door open for a reaffirmation of monsters of epic proportions and a return to the primordial level of civilization evoked in the opening section of the book. Although it seems to point to the future, the pattern formed by the *tesserae* is a gloomy, top-heavy one of cyclical historical regression.

The conversations of Polo and Kan frame the speculations catalyzed by their "emblematic" city descriptions. They also explore the themes that dominate Calvino's thought during this period: for example, the influence on the present of the paths not taken (34–35), the cost of progress (66), and the *gioco combinatorio* (49). In anticipation of the reduction or leveling of human personality traits to their archetypes that occurs in *Il castello dei destini incrociati*, here civilizations are condensed into symbols of themselves. Although Kan's cities may have at one time existed in fact and Polo's are pure abstractions (65), the cities of both men exist only within the confines of Kan's garden and only when evoked through contemplation.

Like Faria, Kan will attempt to write a linear narrative composed of plausible cities, perfect crystals of form, "a model from which all possible cities can be deduced" (75). Polo, on the other hand and like Edmond Dantès, will concentrate on "all possible impossibles" (92), and utilize them to construct a "general system." In addition, the prospect of intellectually comprehending all possible narratives causes Polo, whose voice clearly reflects Calvino's, to ultimately cede his right to narrate ("the ear, not the voice, is in charge of the tale" [143]) and place all responsibility for the construction of the text on the addressee/interpreter. However, once again the reader can narrate only what has been excogitated in the mind of the narrator.

To illustrate, the seventh chapter of *Le città invisibili* is the only one in which the ephemeral interchanges between Polo and Kan take on the icastic physicality of direct dialog. Yet even here the conflation of what exists within and without the mind leads the two to contemplate the reality of a reified system of class exploitation:

> Polo: Perhaps the laborers, the trash collectors, the cooks who clean the guts out of chickens, the washerwomen who slap their laundry on stones, mothers who stir their rice while nursing their babies, exist only because we think of them.
>
> Kublai: To tell you the truth, I never think about them.
>
> Polo: Then they do not exist.

> Kublai: This possibility does not strike me as the most convenient. Without them, you and I would never be able wrap ourselves up in our blankets and sway in our hammocks. [123]

Polo's arrival signals the transition in Kan's empire from an exploitive system that predates the commodification of human labor and the advent of conceptual reasoning. One would assume that the surplus value produced by Kan's laborers, washerwomen, and the others is recorded in the concrete tabulations of number and script. The merchant Polo introduces him to a means of explaining material reality through abstraction: pure thought that does not consider the worker's direct experience of the world. This satisfies Kan's desire for universal norms. Answers to all his questions can now be formulated as timeless conceptual terms. The origin of the social hierarchies and the unhistorical mode of thought that inform the parassitic dominance of the protobourgeois merchant and noble are not interrogated but concealed and mystified so that they will appear eternal. As he relaxes with Kan, everything that Polo sees and does begins to "make sense in an intellectual space" (109). Thought—timeless, axiomatic concepts—then supplants lived experience: no longer does "one know what is on the inside and what is on the outside" (110). Polo's abstract reasoning, which justifies and is justified by the production and exchange of commodities, can then come full circle and assert that human labor exists only because he and Kan exploit it.

Tucked away in the emperor's garden, Kan and Polo can observe without being observed. Thus, in a very real way, what emanates from the discussions between the two "emblems among emblems" is a discourse of power. Because they believe it possible to contain social reality within an intellectual system and dominate it, they symbolically embody the collusion of the ideological superstructure (Polo) and the coercive power of the state (Kan). They reify their dominance through tautological self-authentication: "we have demonstrated that if we did not exist, we would not exist" (*abbiamo dimostrato che se non ci fossimo, non ci saremmo* [123]). Ironically, the intellectual, Polo, while assuaging the warrior-king's repressed traumas and rationalizing the guilt propelling his overlord's nightmares, is completely unaware of the extent of his subservience to the discourse of power he himself constructs and perpetuates.

Subsequent to this complete removal of their conversation from lived experience, the two discuss (in chapters VIII and IX) the act of writing, specifically the creation of fictions more real than reality itself. At this point, all verbal communication between Polo and Kan ceases. Polo—bearer of timeless knowledge, thinker-writer, "mute informer" (127), mandarin who intellectually dominates the infinite and infinitesimal—provides ideological support for Kan's political domination. Kan is frustrated in his search for a plausible arrangement of his chess pieces, a coherent and harmonious system, or "invisible order of cities" (128) but Polo dominates both the macroscopic *combinatoire* and the infinitesimal composition of the board. Kan's atlas reflects the present geopolitical configuration of his empire, composed of many cities that, together, combine to form a whole. Polo's suprahistorical perspective shows him the number of possible reconfigurations are not one but infinite: "the catalog of forms is unending: new cities will continue to be created until each possible form is realized" (146).

Polo's open-ended catalog of forms is a prelude to Palomar's use of enumeration as a means of intellectually mastering the randomness and heterogeneity of the universe. Observation and enumeration or catalogization of phenomena would permit a pattern, or recursive symmetry, to emerge from the chaos and disorder.[2]

Calvino's search was indeed for the ever-elusive "filigree of the universe" (Ups 156). As he made clear in the introductory note to *Una pietra sopra*, his slow withdrawal from active political engagement in the 1950s and 1960s did not preclude his "requisite to try to understand, and indicate and compose." In fact, and in all fairness, it is not possible to underwrite the "pluralistic nonselection" Musarra attributes to him. Nonetheless, the waning of a future-oriented *progettualità* did cast in relief an aspect of his work that he would later claim was present from the outset: "the sense of the complex and of the multiple and of the relative and of the multifaceted" that came to "determine a posture of *systematic* perplexity" (my emphasis; Ups VIII). Doubt and perplexity are utilized by Calvino in an attempt to know and create taxonomies of seemingly random phenomena. His ultimate failure to reach his goals—that is to say, the final prevalence of perplexity over order—does not alter the essential nature of his epistemological project.

III. *Il castello dei destini incrociati*

Le città invisibili and *Il castello dei destini incrociati* mark the transformation of the Calvinian subject from a Crocean one into a phenomenological observer. This evolution takes place with no dramatic interruption or break, because traces of the combinatoric, or metafictional, inquiry that comes to the fore in the early 1970s can be found in his poetics as early as the 1950s. While translating and editing the anthology of *Fiabe italiane* (1956), he was not, he took great pain to stress, "enclosed within the impermeable armor [*catafratto*] of the Crocean distinction between poetry because a poet makes it his own when he re-creates it"—and "that which instead plunges back into an objective, almost vegetal limbo" of nonpoetry" (xiv). Instead, he had in mind, he tells us, the Tuscan proverb which, when paraphrased, says the value of the novella is increased by what is weaved and reweaved onto it each time it is told, from the new that is added to it each time is passes from mouth to mouth. By retelling stories, he became, in his own words, a "link in the anonymous and unending chain by which fables are handed down to posterity, links which are never pure instruments, passive transmitters, but (and here the proverb and Benedetto Croce cross paths) their true authors." And yet, one might ask, if Croce's thought was of minor import, and given Calvino's concern for his public self-image, why did Calvino raise the issue of Croce's influence, only to deny or, at least, downplay it?

While adapting the fables, to close this brief parenthesis, he felt the need to compare and classify them. In fact, in "*Il midollo del leone*," published while he was working on the *Fiabe*, Calvino averred the fables provide "the necessary schema of all human stories" (Ups 15). In other words, in the *Fiabe* we uncover not only a practical application of Croce's distinction between poetry and nonpoetry, but also, and this is what matters in this context, the root of the *combinatoire* of minimal narrative units and the desire to apocryphically reconfigure the canon. Through this process of rearranging, synonymous in his view with the act of narration, subjectivity is constituted. As he wrote, "the fable must be recreated each time, so that at the center of the narration is the man who narrates . . . his personal style and charm. And it is through this person that we gain access to the continuously renewed time between the atemporal fable with the world of its audience" (*Fiabe italiane* xxvii).

In the 1960s, Calvino gradually attributed increased importance the act of writing, and on defining an all-encompassing metafictional totality. Then the self-renewing configurations of combinatorics gave way to the search for an origin, which, in this later period, was to be found in the enduring materiality of the visual image. Calvino identified the origin with the visual image, which in his appraisal preexisted and gave rise to ephemeral spoken and indeterminate written language. What was said of the early Qfwfq, I write, therefore I am, would in effect be corrected to I see, therefore I write. The constitutive element of Crocean subjectivity, artistic intuition, was supplanted by the supraindividual archetypes of metafiction. They, in turn, would give way to a material world recuperable through sight. The point of arrival is the visual image, which supplies humanity with its phenomenological link to materiality and makes the word possible. Indeed, in Calvino's *Lezione* on visibility, a hierarchy is established in which priority over the written text is given to the visual image, considered the fount of literary creation. Literature, in this scheme of things, can develop the most complicated of concepts, but only after taking its spark from an image.

Il castello dei destini incrociati is written at a time when ekphrastic investigation comes to support and complement metafictional combinatorics in Calvino's poetic inquiry, prior to the assertion of phenomenological defamiliarization. *Se una notte d'inverno un viaggiatore* (1979), the only major work of prose published by Calvino in the interlude between *Il castello* and *Palomar*, will stand as a final aftereffect of the postulated metafictional *grand récit*.

In contrast to the open-endedness of Polo's cities, the *Castello* depicts two self-contained systems, which allow for reconfigurations, but brook no addition of new elements. Subtending *Il castello* is the implicit equivalence of the mythological archetypes and minimal narrative units generated by the tarots; the deck is a totality that contains an infinite number of possible narrative combinations. Hence the imbrication of metafiction and ekphrasis: the tarots are the material representations of both human archetypes and of what Frye has called "the constitutive elements of story-telling" (51). For Motte, the cards are literally and metaphorically marginal to the text (126). However, it is imperative we also keep in mind their fundamental role as the inspiration or catalyst for narration.[3] In fact, if *Il castello* is read in the light of "*Il romanzo come spettacolo*" (Ups 217–20), written three years earlier, we may begin to understand how the visual image gained increasing importance in Calvino's thought, at the expense of the written word. Part of this essay deals with the illustrations Dickens commissioned for inclusion into certain of his novels. In the works cited by Calvino, the graphic images are in a decidedly subaltern position with respect to the written text. However, Calvino stresses that Dickens's "histrionic passion" (216) not only led him to reestablish a link between the novel and the oral tradition, but also, through the use of illustrations in his texts, to "direct [his public's] visual interpretation" of his works (217). If a lost physical bond (grounded in the presence of the spoken word and in the materiality of the image) between writer and audience could be reestablished, modern narration, just as in the mythical times of the epic storyteller (*cantastorie* or *favoleggiatore*), could once again be a *spettacolo collettivo* and the aural-oral image would regain priority over the written word.

Contemporaneously, the recuperation of the artisanal aspects of narration identified in this brief article—the framing tale utilized in classic narratives such as the *Decameron*, the *Arabian Nights*, and the *Canterbury Tales* on the one hand and on the other the analysis of the fundamental structures of narrative—provide the basic building blocks of the *Castello*.

In his "*Autobiografia di uno spettatore*" (1974), Calvino deals more directly with archetypes and with the concept of pure observation or defamiliarization. By his own account, as an adolescent in the early 1930s he was an assiduous frequenter of the San Remo movie theaters. During those years, he attempted to use film to compile a taxonomy, "a human typology," of his fellow viewers (XIV). These abstract character traits are essentially the archetypes that inform the *Le cosmicomiche*, *Le città invisibili*, and *Il castello dei destini incrociati*. As an adult Calvino wished to re-create the sensation of being a "pure spectator" (XIX). He would go to the movies hoping that the movie screen would dilate "the boundaries of reality" (XVIII) and force him "to observe what the naked eye tends to skip over without pause" (XIX). The point of arrival of such ruminations will be the "phenomenological approach to the world" or the "estrangement effect in literature" later described in detail by Calvino in "The Written and Unwritten Word" (1983).[4] Only defamilarization would make possible the reacquisition of that sense of distance, necessary for the construction an "abstract space," that, as he put it, "allows us to begin to understand ourselves" ("Autobiografia di uno spettatore" XX).[5]

Following Frye (in the 1969 essay "*La letteratura come proiezione del desiderio*" [Ups 195–203]), Calvino describes human desire as "a force that guides human society as it develops its own idiosyncratic form" (195) and then claims to have begun to "to seek nonmystifying ways of reading literature that cut deeper to the heart of their object" (196): by going directly from the individual mind and its immediate context to the origins of the universe, he can accept—because they are in his opinion eternally human—certain moral categories such as good, evil, greed, will to dominate. He rejects "historicist readings"—which he implies are mystificatory—that consider the "outside" of the text (201) so he can explore their internal workings. This, he claims, grants him "unexpected insight" into the "centripetal motion" of the work. The text's "centripetal motion" makes it the center of gravity of a "bibliocentric universe," which in his definition is "a selection of books lined up on a shelf to whom is given a particular global value and around which all other possible books are organized" (202).

Much like Dantès's prison, his "ideal library," he continues, "is the one that gravitates outward, towards apocryphal works, in the etymological sense, that is toward hidden works . . . the new aprocyphal text to be found or invented" (203). Following Frye, within the literary realm staked out by Calvino, the catalyst for the reconfiguration of the canon would be human desire. If we put aside the significance of this assertion for the reading of specific texts by Calvino, particularly in light of the central importance of the word *apocrifo* in *Se una notte d'inverno un viaggiatore*, and for Calvino's perspective on his own work as a writer, we can see the deep bond for Calvino between writing, the return to the origins of the universe, and the search for a human quintessence. Calvino's quest is for a *primum mobile* that would provide a key for the decipering and mastering of a metanarrative.

In three essays collected in *Una pietra sopra* (and associated under the common heading "Definition of Territories") Calvino stakes out the limits of human quintessence. In his essay on eroticism, sex, and laughter (1969, Ups 211–14) he avers that the center of human existence, sexual desire, defies representation. Because he saw a deep anthropological bond between sex and laughter (the latter is defined as a defense mechanism "for dominating the absolute turmoil sex can provoke" [212]), he claimed that laughter serves to indicate and "recognize the limit one is about to cross, the entrance into a diverse, paradoxical, sacred space" (212). Similarly, since desire cannot be clinically analyzed, Calvino chooses to respond to the "terribleness (*terribilità*) of living" (214) by using comedy to attack the "thick symbolic armor under which Eros hides" (211). He cites his own "Cosmicomiche" as a use of comedy, specifically the incongruity of nonanthropomorphic amorous relationships, as one means of going outside the human in order to capture the quintessentially human. As he specified in the first of this suite of essays, "through [comedy] we reach the sort of *distancing from the particular, the sense of the vastness of the totality*" (157, my emphasis).[6]

To return to *Il castello*, the subject of narration begins interpreting and re-presenting the tarots to the reader as soon as he enters (16). As the suite advances diegetically, the stories emanate from a set of basic units. Contemporaneously, the immanent narrator is absorbed into the archetypes and ultimately becomes an archetype himself, an everyman who is unable to find his own autobiography among the cards.[7]

The self-effacement of the writing subject is particularly apparent in the introductory tale of the "Tavern" suite. In the "Tavern" Calvino once again elevates his own autobiography to a symbolic level; the autobiographical subtext comes to underpin and frame the entire group. It is of special importance within three of the tales: the first, that of the indecisive young man who loses himself in a Borgesian garden of forking paths, that of the writer (Faust-Parcifal), and the concluding tale (Saints Jerome and George).

"*L'indeciso*" arrives in "*la Città del Tutto*" only to learn that even plenitude is contingent on choice and refusal (59). Like Calvino, he must choose between art and social engagement. Unable to decide (and convinced of the impossibility of reconciling the two callings within himself, he uncovers a tarot that represents both the cosmos and the sea, where "the acquatic origins of life are celebrated" (60). He chooses to avert his gaze from the sea and look toward outer space, where the planet's past and future are encapsulated. From that vantage he can distinguish a humanity that is "waste of material that is going to ruin," and a cosmos that is an amalgam of atoms that does nothing but "repeat that which has happened inside constellations . . . for billions of years" (60). The narrator then encounters the sinister guardian angel of the forking paths who forces him to contemplate the world that will survive the death of humanity:

> If the only thing he wanted was to escape from individual limitations, categories, roles, to hear the thunder that roars inside molecules, the mixing of raw and final materials, here is the road that opens up before him . . . each species and individual and the entire history of humanity are nothing more than an accidental link in a chain of mutations and evolutions. [62]

A future of decomposition and the reaffirmation of the mineral substance of the planet closes a historical cycle and returns matter to the origin whence it, and humanity, came.

The immanent narrator understands that the question of being and nonbeing can be understood, but only within the larger nonanthropocentric and cosmic contexts.

The pendant to this tale is "*Due storie in cui si cerca e ci si perde*" where, once again, the autobiographical writing subject becomes an archetype of all writers and writing a metaphor for human existence. Although the third autobiographical tale of "*La taverna*," "*Anch'io cerco di dire la mia*," is the more often cited by critics, it is foreshadowed by "*Due storie in cui si cerca e ci si perde*." The title is significantly ambiguous. It can be rendered in English as "one looks and gets lost," or as "we look and get lost." This ambivalence adumbrates the archetypal nature of the tale, which discusses the immanent narrator's life in terms that parallel yet supersede Calvino's biography to approach a transcendental human condition. The elderly immanent narrator, "dedicated the best years of his life to [a] great work" whose implied goal was that of "liberating himself from egoisms and individual limitations, of becoming one with the forces that move the foundation of things." This "great work," like the tarot deck, would contain all stories. Unfortunately, "just when it seems he has successfully fit into place everyone else's stories, he realizes his own has been lost" (90).

The story of the elderly writer intertwines with that of a young warrior whose strength is "so new to the world, and so preoccupied by his being in the world that he neglects to ask about what he sees" (96). Thus, the autobiographical resonances evoke a path abandoned by Calvino—that of active political militancy—while oscillating between "*il tutto e il nulla*" ("all and nothing" [97]). The tale of the young warrior looks back to an origin, the nothingness that preexists the individual, while the elder narrator looks forward into the *combinatoire* of continuously self-reconfiguring matter that coincides with his future nonbeing.

The conclusion of "*Anch'io cerco di dire la mia*"—a story that explicitly confuses the immanent narrator, the autobiographical, the writer's condition, and a universal human need to combat the enemy without while keeping at bay the enemy within—comes as anticlimactic after the discussion of the act of writing in which the narrator affirms that writing is nothing more than "sleight of hand consisting of putting the tarots in line and extracting stories from them" (105). The contribution of the single writer is predetermined and limited: "writing has a substratum (*sottosuolo*) that belongs to the species" (103); the narrating *I* quickly understands:

> Perhaps the moment has arrived to admit that the first tarot is the only one that can represent honestly that which I have succeeded in becoming: a juggler or conjurer who arranges on his sideshow table a certain number of figures and by moving them around, connecting them, and substituting for them creates a certain number of special effects. [105]

All that is individual is leveled; the writing subject, a mere *bricoleur*, is negated. The writer is reduced to metafictional archetype, an emblem among the emblems.

The ebb of the importance of metafictional combinatorics in Calvino's poetics is signaled in the final paragraph of the concluding "Nota." As he wrote: "my theoretical and expressive interest for these experiments has run out. It is time (from all points of view) to move on" (128). And so he looks to an origin, to a time prior to writing, when human subjectivity was constituted through its interpretation of the visual image.

IV. Ekphrasis

The term *ekphrastic hope* has been used to designate the writer's desire to merge with the semantic other (Mitchell 702). Ekphrastic envy, then, may be defined as the desire to be subsumed by the semiotic other, to negate the writing subject through subordination to the pictorial text. When analyzing ekphrastic texts, we must carefully examine how image and word interact and then determine whether the literary and graphic texts complement one another, or if a subaltern text merely supplements the dominant one. That is to say, we must attempt to determine whether ekphrastic hope or envy underpins the text.

While it is true that "the supplement is in fact what *allows the privileged term to be constituted*" (Hayles 182, her emphasis), only the establishment of a relationship of equality between the literary and the graphic can enable the writer or artist to overcome the traditional definition of a work as the expression of an interiority, undermine any pretense of unitary meaning, and approach a continually self-transforming plurality of visions.

In Calvino's ekphrastic writings, image and word do not complement one another in a relationship of parity, nor do they work to undermine traditional hierarchies by approaching a more collective form of artistic production.[8] By accepting as somehow more *real* a flattened, two-dimensional representation, whether it is the static vision of the graphic artist or the monocular vision of the cinema, Calvino eschews any interrogative exchange between writing and visual media. In Calvino's ekphrastic writings, word and image come to share a single dominant perspective—based on the subalternity of the word to the image it describes or interprets—that works to restore the referential status of the image. As we shall see, underlying Calvino's inquiry is the failure to note the extent to which social reality impinges on all interpretations of physical reality. This will ultimately lead Palomar to reify the observing subject's interpretation of physical reality.

"*La squadratura*" (1975), Calvino's introduction to a volume of photographic reproductions of paintings by Giulio Paolini, forecefully signals the shift in Calvino's poetics from combinatoric investigation (after its failure—announced at the conclusion of *Castello dei destini in-*

crociati—to provide Calvino with a metanarrative) to an ekphrastic search for a material referent. Foremost in Calvino's mind, at this point in time, is the identification of an unmoveable point of reference. How does one, he asks, "stick to the things of which one can be certain, which are very few, and look at them with faith and sympathy, at least for a fleeting moment"? ("*La squadratura*" VII).

He responds that the painter, unlike the writer, shares with the addressee of the artistic message a common ground provided by the objective materiality of the painting. The writer, in contrast, comes into contact with the reader only through the linguistic indeterminacy of the text. The referent for Calvino is no longer the material object of representation but instead the plastic image. He confuses material reality and its representations, thereby ignoring the signifying processes through which materiality is filtered. Thus, the writer Calvino's ekphrastic envy—or, as he phrased it elsewhere, "the writer's eternal insuppressible envy of the painter" (Cds 76)—leads him to assert, "the writer too would like to produce works this way" ("*La squadratura*" VII), that is, with the benefit of a more material medium; he would like to employ, as does the painter, "the material object that is the painting" (VII).

Calvino's ruminations lead him to contemplate a totalizing work, distinguished by "an absolute impersonality" (X), that would include the canvas, the horizontal eye-level field of view, other members of the gallery public, and the painter who is no longer the artificer but an element of the composition: "photographed while he unveils his work" (X). Once subsumed within the work, the painter can identify with an atemporal "painting *I*," composed not only of the collective *I* of the great painters of the past, but with "the potentialities within the field of painting" (X): the works of the future that already exist as possibilities within the medium. Calvino then briefly contemplates a totality of all immaginable perspectives that would include what is seen by the depicted. In this way, the watcher would see him/herself through the eyes of the watched. But this possibility is quickly discarded. The only perspective the dispassionate observer can identify with, according to Calvino, is a unifying, objective one, that of "an eye suspended over the world."

To Calvino's mind, the relationship between the writer and the world, because of the indeterminacy of language, is much more problematic than that of the painter. The writer is deprived of the immediate contact between self and world available to practitioners of that sister art. The materiality of painting, as Calvino uses the term, effectively overcomes the deferral of meaning between signifier and signified, and the consequent semantic multiplicity of language.[9] The materiality of painting, on the other hand, allows the painter to approach a unifying discourse: "the painter tends to reduce the multiple to the singular, the writer, perhaps, does the opposite" ("*La squadratura*" XIII). Because of this, the painter can avoid both expressionistic representations of the irrational self and impressionistic, lyric autobiographism and "communicate," a verb to which Calvino attributed a univocity that surmounted both the subjectivity of expression and the *difference* between signifier and signified, and, as a consequence, permitted the exchange of pure referents.

In "*La squadratura*," Calvino avers that the referentiality of the medium allows the painter to approach a supraindividual or archetypal status—to become the expression of "the collective *I* of the great painters of the past" (X)—endowed with an "absolute impersonality" (X). To use Calvino's phrasing, the "painter's metaphysic and his *chosisme*" (concentration or focus on objects)[10] are one and the same: "objects, the tools of the trade, the acts of painting (beginning with *sight*) are, for the painter the only *absolutes*" (XII). The integration of the artist within this "absolute pictorial work" or visual totality, in Calvino's words, is "the ultimate end or goal of art" (IX). Calvino's envy of the painter and of painting derives from his desire to escape from the relativity or heterogeneity characteristic of the postmodern condition (and much more specifically, the indeterminate, polysemantic nature of his own medium of artistic expression) and return to a bedrock of absolutes.

For Herman postmodernism embraces competing representations of reality, which cannot be placed in a hierarchy by appealing to a univocal material referent. Knowledge, he claims, can be grounded only in the "arbitration of competing views" (76). However, in Calvino's appraisal the visual image furnishes a univocal material referent that would enable the writer to communicate. He ignores that the graphic art he (re)presents in his ekphrastic works is open to interpretations other than his own. Moreover, he does not see the indeterminacy of writing as potentially emancipating. Instead it renders that medium of expression inferior to its sister art, painting, which is endowed with materiality.

Calvino wished to use ekphrasis to move beyond the inherent "inferiority" of writing and utilize the materiality of the painted image as a source of inspiration. He hoped it would provide the writer with an orienting totality, "a geometrical grid . . . that contains all paintings" (XIV). In his words:

> The photographs of his divided (*squadrata*) canvas can fill the catalog of an imaginary art museum; they can be repeated many times but attributed to imaginary painters, and given the titles of possible and impossible paintings, titles that would force the viewer to look at them carefully.
>
> When the writer looks at these paintings, he reads in them the *incipit* of countless volumes, the library of apocryphal works that he would like to write (XIV).

The image exists prior to the word. It provides the inspiration for new works of literature, which, in effect, merely scamble and reassemble combinatorically previously utilized, basic narrative units recuperated from a Borgesian library of Babel.

In *Il castello* ekphrasis and combinatorics form a metafictional totality. Minimal narrative units are recycled by the writing *bricoleur* into a textual totality. As Calvino wrote in his review of the translation of Frye's *Anatomy of Criticism*:

> Literature is comprised not only of single works but also of libraries or systems in which various periods and traditions organize "canonical" and "apocryphal" texts. Within these systems each work is different from how it would be if isolated or included in another library. A library can have a closed catalog or it can tend to become universal, but always while expanding around a nucleus of "canonical" books. That nucleus, more than the catalog, is the center of gravity that distinguishes one library from another. The ideal library toward which I tend is the one that gravitates toward the outside, toward "apocryphal" works, in the etymological sense of the word, that is to say, toward "hidden" works. Literature is a search for the book hidden far away, that changes the value of books that are already known. It is the tension toward the new apocryphal text to be found or invented. [Ups 202–3]

Thus when the narrating voice of "*La squadratura*" claims that "painting is both a totality to which nothing can be added and a potentiality that implicates all that is paintable" (XIV), he is equating painting with the libraries just mentioned. These "libraries" contain all books, including those that exist as potentialities but have yet to be written. The basic elements of narrative, archetypal human character traits and conflictual situations, can be reexplored and rearranged, but nothing new can be invented. So we see that for Calvino writing becomes a search for potentialities within a preexisting totality, a reformulation of the basic elements of a given medium of expression. Whereas Qfwfq traced *segni nello spazio* as a way of manifesting his subjectivity to then subordinate that constructed identity to its relative space/time coordinates, the Calvinian subject now gives proof of its existence through its ability to intervene and catalyze modifications in a preexisting totality.

The graphic sign, the element common to both drawing and writing, is no longer simply a means of expression and hence a manifestation of subjectivity. It now comes to supplant the artist who, because of ekphrastic envy, is reduced to object of the creative act. The graphic signs placed by the writer on the page are the material link between the writer and the written, but more important, they—not the author—are the agent of the text. Unlike Qfwfq who, in "*Un segno nello spazio*," utilized graphic expression to constitute identity (I am, therefore I write), the only proof this *I* has that it exists is what it has written (I write, therefore I am).

When writing is defined as the act of reconfiguring extant "bibliographic universes" and the production of "apocryphal" works, the writer may make no claim to agency. The author/*bricoleur* is "dead" in the Barthesian sense of the term. And just as the work sets its sights solely on the reformulation of its medium, the artist foresakes social commitment and aims exclusively on self–redefinition. Paradoxically, Calvino claims that the artist, having placed the graphic line on a page, "is finally master of the world," mover or catalyst of the totality, "even though he cannot escape from a shared condition of prisoner" ("*La penna in prima persona*" Ups 295). Much like his "Count of Montecristo," this writer is intellectual lord of the prison that holds him/her captive. Furthermore, the *I* claims to be "its own master" because it maintains control over its own state of being and/or nonbeing:

> The only way out the writing *I* has left is that of killing itself with two ink lines; it will then discover that death-erasure is made of the same substance as life-drawing. Both are a movement of the pen on the sheet. [295]

Being and nonbeing are cut from the same cloth and both are dependent on the drawn/written line. Freedom, then, is the acknowledgment and understanding of non-being," or Borges's hide behind, what he will refer to in "*Forse un mattino andando*" as a Montalean void. Through writing the author overtakes nothingness, the condition of never having existed or of having existed only as potentiality, and enters into the flow of being into nonbeing.

The artist/prisoner is transformed by the *opera totale* from artificer to artifact, at once *espositore, esposto e pubblico* ("the displayer, the display, and the public"; 298). The artist exists, but only because the work exists. Whereas the work was once superfluous expression—the external manifestation of intuition—it now authenticates the artist's very being. The *uomo-linea*, or object of writing and drawing, can do no more than condition the formal evolution of a prison, what is "drawn and drawable." It can then hope to reach, in Calvino's words, "the true proof of the *I*'s existence, its *ergo sum*" ("*La penna in prima persona*," Ups 296).

Thus, ekphrastic investigation is for Calvino a means of defining the act of writing, which in turn is the only proof of the subject's identity. In fact, in "*I livelli della realtà in letteratura*" (1978; Ups 310–23), Calvino states:

> "I write." This affirmation is the first and only given reality the writer can use as a point of departure. "At this moment I am writing." This is the same as saying: "You who read, may—must—only believe one thing: what you are reading is something that someone wrote in the past . . . You would be mistaken if you thought that reading put you in direct contact with the experience of realms that do not coincide with that of the written word." [312]

I write and you read me, therefore we both exist. The author exists only through the sign. However, neither the subjectivity of the writer nor that of the reader is contingent on dialog with the writing or reading other. If they look at each other at all, they do so as voyeurs, neither desiring nor expecting their gazes to be reciprocated. The text is not the space of a Blanchotian meeting in absentia, but instead the coincidental encounter of writer and reader monologs. Moreover, since reality is literary—only what is recounted in texts exists; shared real, worldly, extratextual experience is discounted—the author's fictive world is self-authenticating.

In the 1960s Qfwfq believed the world's existence was contingent on his own. Now the Calvinian subject realizes that the world enjoys an autonomous existence. Writing is no longer the external, superfluous manifestation of intuition, but a means of reconfiguring the world and of authenticating identity. However, if this is to take place, the subject must negate itself and allow itself to be absorbed into a totality or unifying discourse.

This process was first begun in the combinatoric writing of the early 1970s, *Le città invisibili* and *Il castello dei destini incrociati*. In these works the intellectual/writer was transformed through abstraction into the archetype or symbol of itself. The ekphrastic subordination of indeterminate writing to material painting, the use of the visual image as a source of inspiration, brings the author one step closer to the prospected master narrative. Once the author has been reduced to symbol, s/he ceases to be the subject of artistic creation. S/he can reconfigure a preexisting totality, thereby verifying his/her own existence, but only as the object of the graphic lines placed on the page.

V. Writing

Through the mid-1960s and beyond, despite a sincere and suffered social engagement, Calvino's vision was subject-centered. Propelling the writing subject into the surrounding environ was the moral tension evident in his nonfiction. In the poetics of the "*midollo del leone*" the

Crocean equation of "poetry" or the aesthetically "beautiful" with an ethical tension coincided with the centrality of the moral individual in narrative and the desire to safeguard it within mass society. In turn, the moral fiber of the subject of narrative was to emanate throughout society. To use his phrasing, "in every real poetry there exists a lion's marrow, nourishment for a rigorous morality, for a mastery of history" (Ups 17).

The equation of this moral tension with the "poetic" or esthetically "beautiful" subtends "*La sfida al labirinto*" (1962; Ups 82–97), an essay in which the importance of the subject causes Calvino to reject out of hand those schools of thought—such as existentialism, phenomenology, and psychoanalytic theory—which deal with "interiorities." Calvino can move toward a phenomenological vision only when he is convinced he can utilize it to analyze exteriorities, that is to say, the universe of objects and the individual's place among them. Paradoxically, at the heart of this inquiry is a search for and description of essences, those of the subject and of what surrounds it in space and in time. However, Calvino's probe falls far short of establishing dialogic bonds with "other myselves," as we shall see.

His homage to Montale, "*Forse un mattino andando*" (1977), marks an important road mark in Calvino's intellectual biography. In this essay he cites one of the Nobel laureate's *ossi di seppia* ("*Forse un mattino andando in un'aria di vetro*") as an example of a "case in which subjective experience of space is separated from experience of the objective world." In Calvino's reading of the poem, the *I* separates empirical space into what is seen and the unseen void behind the subject. The world is divided into the visible foreground, defined as a *schermo d'inganni* (a deceitful screen), and the nothingness at our back, the nonexistence that for him constitutes "the true substance of the world."

Calvino then ingeniously develops this thought, by citing with tongue in cheek a "fundamental anthropological revolution of our century": the implementation of the rearview mirror in automobiles. It must be noted that Calvino is quick to distinguish the rearview mirror from those that objectify the subject by including it in the field of vision. "The mirror," he writes, "confirms the presence of the observing subject, for whom the world is an accessory background." In contradistinction, the rearview mirror excludes the observer from the field of vision. Indeed, the motorist can be considered "a new biological species" because of it: the driver "can comprehend in a single glance two opposing (*contrapposti*) visual fields without the encumbrance of his own image, as if he were no more than an eye suspended over the totality of the world."

In his reading of "*Forse andando in un'aria di vetro*," Calvino sees Montale dividing humanity into those who consider only empirical reality and those who also acknowledge what can be seen through a metaphorical rearview mirror: Borges's "hide-behind" or the void of nonbeing. For Calvino the acknowledgment and acceptance of nonbeing is "true knowledge." This quest for "true knowledge," as we will see, will be intimately linked to the dénouement of *Palomar*, when the protagonist imagines himself dead. At any rate, in "*Forse un mattino andando*" Calvino finds the strength of Montale's lyrics in the poet's acknowledgment of both the "foreground" (an "empirical world" perceived as a cinematic "optical illusion," a two-dimensional representation of three-dimensionality) and the "background" (the understanding that the counterpart of this optical illusion is the nonworld or "hide-behind," the nothingness at one's back).

For Calvino, the "fundamental point" of the poem is found in Montale's ability to go "forward enraptured with the morning air," while acknowledging the silent void that protects "the secret seized in the lightning-swift" moment of intuition. In "*Forse un mattino andando*," once the subject is able to view the world through a rearview mirror, so to speak, once it is convinced it has been granted 360° vision, the subject can contemplate the world from the outside, not as a part of it. The individual can quietly go toward the void of nonbeing, "the nothingness, the void we know is the Alpha and the Omega of everything."

5 Calvino: The Master Narrative

I. Between the Infinite and the Infinitesimal

Ferretti underscores the "political lucidity, civil passion and intellectual coherence and faith in democracy" that underpin Calvino's writings during the 1970s (114). He sees these partially overtaken by "signs of a pessimism not entirely attributable to the Italian crisis (the student uprisings of 1977, terrorism, the Moro assassination, et cetera)." Ferretti also identifies a tendency in Calvino to "decompose the *totality* in *multiplicities*." Thus, in his view "cataloging" or "collecting" are for Calvino a means of regulating the arbitrariness of existence (144). "In *Palomar*'s narrative structure of juxtaposed mosaic tiles," he specifies, "Calvino realizes with extreme rigor the convergence of his 'predilection for geometric forms, for symmetries, for series' . . . and of his renunciation of a global design and of a social project" (143–44).

I agree with Ferretti's general thesis that the "challenge to the labyrinth"—that is, the vehement defense of the individual threatened with drowning in the "sea of objectivity"—launched by Calvino on the pages of Vittorini's *Menabò* in the early 1960s increasingly became an unwillingness to intervene until the world could be dominated by the intellect. However, I would also contend that while—as Ferretti argues—Calvino did in fact move decidedly away from any future-oriented project, the writer's microscopic observations, his *petits récits*, were part of an albeit unsuccessful attempt to recompose reality into a global design. The *tesserae*--as Calvino described them, "a cross between the apologue and the *petit poème en prose*" (*Lezioni americane* 56)—which inform *Palomar* organize themselves into a diegetic whole.

The nonanthropocentric perspective first experimented in *Le cosmicomiche* allows Calvino in *Palomar* to place the self squarely at the center of an analysis of the infinite and the infinitesimal. In his own words, "*Palomar* complements *Le cosmicomiche*, a work in which I expounded on the infinite nature of the universe in a way that was both abstract and imaginative. In *Palomar* I look at minute things directly and close up" (Mauro). While the "old" Qfwfq availed himself of a telescope, Palomar looks at the world through a microscope, limits his participation in massified society and becomes evermore a nonparticipating observer. At the same time, he tries to utilize the nonanthropocentric perspective of *Le cosmicomiche* to identify humanity's essence.

Fundamental to his analysis of the infinitesimal is the abstraction through inductive reasoning of a grand narrative. His use of *mathesis singularis*[1] or catalogization, the phenomenological description of the world and the enumeration of those descriptions, was to provide the basis for a "general solution." Palomar's perplexity, Calvino notes, was not due to a lack of faith in a unifying system. Instead it derives from the frustration caused by an inability to capture and describe essences (Mauro) necessary for the reconstruction of a metanarrative.

II. Mathesis Singularis

In his *Lezione americana* dedicated to "Exactitude" Calvino rhapsodized on the concept of *mathesis singularis*, arguing that solutions to specific problems when taken together can lead to a general solution" (*Lezioni americane* 73). Critical writings on Calvino have put this increased propensity to examine the microscopic and to then create *tasselli* or *petits récits* clearly in relief. Following the writer's own explicit declarations, critics have for the most part discounted any macroscopic tendency within the combinatory play of the later narratives. However, Calvino's own explanation of the manner in which he appropriated the intellectual tradition of the Enlightenment contradicts such hypotheses and relates to his use of *mathesis singularis*.

In *Collezione di sabbia* Calvino identifies what for him were the two major aspects of "the culture of the luminaries." The first direction of Enlightenment inquiry was that of a unilinear and unifying encyclopedic knowledge. The other was to figure as a fundamental element of Calvino's poetics in the 1980s, specifically, the "detailed knowledge of diversity and of their causes" (41). Thus, it becomes increasingly clear that neither Calvino's "perplexity," nor his insistence on the microscopic necessarily forswears the postulation of a unifying discourse. Rather, as he averred, Palomar's "drama is to be found precisely in his inability to develop his own unique, unitary discourse" (Ramondino). Although Palomar's vision of the totality does in fact remain fragmented into so many *tesserae*, his intent was to eventually abstract and construct from them a *grand récit* from the phenomena observed.

Therefore, understanding of the relationship between the elusive metanarrative and the myriad *petits récits* of which Palomar's intellectual biography is composed becomes increasingly necessary. Cannon notes that in *Collezione di sabbia* "Calvino hopes that by abstracting the sand from the confused winds of lived experience we can begin to understand and construct a model of the world" ("Italo Calvino" 61). Indeed, there is a tension toward systematicity in Calvino's perplexity. Behind the chaos and indeterminacy is a project whose ultimate goal is the intellectual (re)construction of a model of the world.

Following the example of Lévi-Strauss, Calvino would adopt an investigative method that would allow him to ambitiously seek out "the existence of a foundation or a code that inheres in all codes [and] articulates all manifestations of the human, and, beyond the human all living things" ("L'etnologo bifronte"). The question, as Calvino phrased it, was how does one "intercept the secret language of nature, the primordial grammar, the code that is hidden in sundry forms of matter." The inductive method suggested to him by the French anthropologist, particularly its "scrupulous fidelity to the multiplicity of the real," was to be the tool used to arrive at a general set of laws or abstractions, "a reductive schematization." The lesson to be learned from Lévi-Strauss—in opposition to the deductive Stalinism of his youth (which in this light is seen as a general system applied aprioristically—and coercively—to local microcosms)—is that *on ne fait pas une societé à partir d'une système*. The system is the point of arrival, not of departure. Calvino never abandons his search for a totality, but instead opts for an inductive over a deductive method.

The system or totality thus constructed organizes sensory perceptions in an intellectual paradigm. In a lecture contemporaneous to the compilation of *Palomar* and *Collezione di sabbia*, Calvino claims we habitually and unwittingly "read" or abstract the world, "breaking down everything we see into minimal elements, assembling them in meaningful segments, discovering all around us regularities, differences, recurrences, exceptions, substitutions, redundancies" ("The Written and the Unwritten Word" 39). He proposes as an alternative to this state of affairs a phenomenological bridge between self and world to be forged through a process of defamiliarization or estrangement. To this end, he would describe material reality, thinking only "insofar as [one] sees . . . mistrust[ing] every thought coming . . . by any other means" (39).

Had Calvino lived to complete it, *Sotto il sole giaguaro* was to have used all five senses in a phenomenological search for a postulated human essence. As Calvino states in the "Avvertenza" that follows the text, he planned to write five stories and call the volume *I cinque sensi* (95). In other words, his intent was to embrace all of existence within a scheme predetermined by human capacities of perception. As it stands the work includes three stories, dedicated to smell, hearing, and taste. "*Un re in ascolto*" and "*Il nome, il naso*" both deal with senses that have become less acute over time because the survival of the species is no longer dependent on them.

"*Il nome, il naso*" depicts "the noseless man of the future" (11) who can only stand by while "the perfumes of memory evaporate" (15). The author speaks to the prospect of giving new life to "our deaf nostrils" and of returning to a time when odors were not yet "inarticulate" and "illegible," but the inadequacy of the olfactory is implied by the use of synesthesia. In "*Un re in ascolto*" the political power of a monarch confines him to his throne and makes him victim of sensory depravation. Like Edmond Dantès, he would like to "think the palace in each of its parts" (75). However, hearing alone is an inadequate compass. Because he must rely exclusively on his sense of hearing, the king is quickly disoriented: he loses his sense of time (or his "calendar of sounds" [71]) and of space (79ff.). "Is there a story," he asks, "that binds one noise to the next?" The reliance on the auditory deprives the king of the space/time coordinates necessary for the creation of a narrative.

On the other hand, the sense of taste preserves the atavistic vestiges of now latent cannibalistic tendencies, traits that are made manifest in life-sustaining acts such as eating and sexual embrace. In the eponymous story, "*Sotto il sole giaguaro*," the aphrodisiac quality of food (40) is emphasized, linking the instinctual drives for individual and collective survival to those of nourishment and reproduction. The synesthesia that is a necessary element of all three stories seems to indicate that for Calvino no single sensory organ—with the possible, and notable, exception of sight—can phenomenologically master the surrounding environment. "*Sotto il sole giaguaro*" is occasioned by a visual stimulus, that of the "Florentine Codex" of fra'Bernardino di Sahagun. It was originally conceived, Calvino tells us, as "a vast encyclopedia of the knowledge, rites, and daily life of the Aztecs" (63). The encyclopedic compendium of a radically diverse society—in Calvino's own words, "the most dissimilar" and "distant met by Europe in its path toward domination"—affords the narrator the opportunity to consider life in the present from a phenomenologically defamiliarized perspective. In the epigraph the sense of taste is defined as a sort of intuitive knowledge that predates the oral-aural parameters of spoken communication. It is both a "wisdom" ("*sapienza*") that predates all "learning" (*scienza*) and the "origin of experience," in need of no ulterior reflection.

To taste, we are told, is to understand almost instinctively, "without purpose or intent, and without later reflection." However, contemplation of what has been tasted may spark "an idea, the genesis of experience." Thus, the narrating *I* of the story unwittingly seeks out a form of instinctual knowledge within latent atavistic tendencies, which date back to a time when humanity did not see itself as distinct from nature and had not yet begun to interpret its surroundings.[2]

III. Encyclopedic Knowledge

As Calvino told an interviewer, his original goal while writing *Palomar* was to write a sort of encyclopedia (Mauro). It was to have been his individual contribution to the project he assigned to literature of encyclopedically embracing all knowledge:

> Since science no longer trusts general explanations and solutions that are not sectorial and specialized, the great challenge literature faces is that of knowing how to weave together the various branches of knowledge and codes into a manifold and multifaceted vision of the world." [*Lezioni americane* 123]

In other words, literature was called on to do what science could no longer accomplish: bring together multiple microcosms into a compendium of human knowledge and experience, as guarantor of "a nonpartial truth" (127).

Literature is thus seen as "a vast net" (134) which strongly resembles a set of Cartesian coordinates whose every point coincides with those of "the unicum which is the *self* of the writer." Each "unicum" he specified is, "a combinatoria of experiences," "an encyclopedia, a library where everything can be constantly reshuffled and reordered in every possible way" (134–35).

Thus, the project of the mature Calvino becomes that of identifying the essential nature of these small narratives to then use what has been learned to construct a general system. In *Castello di sabbia* this was to be induced from the traces of a primordial or mythic origin rediscovered during Calvino's archeological excursions to the Middle East, Japan, and Mexico.

In the first section of *Collezione di sabbia*, "*Esposizioni, esplorazioni*," the reader accompanies Calvino on a series of anthropological excursions through museum exhibitions. The implied goal of these jaunts is the discovery of a grounding discourse. While examining a collection of samples of sand gathered from points all over the globe, he is reminded of all he has written and hopes the basic building blocks of the earth and of knowledge, sand and words, will somehow provide a "foundation and a model" (13). This quest is complicated by our inability to truly see things, "as if for the first time," with an outlook unprejudiced by preexisting paradigms: "we too could pass by phenomena we had never seen before and not notice them, because our eyes and our minds are used to choosing and registering only that which fits into established categories" (15). He then wonders out loud how one might go beyond inherited modes of seeing and "render conceptually definable that which was and remains *difference*" (21).

In the final section of *Collezione di sabbia*, "*La forma del tempo*," Calvino explores the passage of time through visual traces of ancient civilizations surviving in the present. In the Tokyo train station he is able to see things "as if for the first time." But, he hastens to add, he knows he will quickly grow accustomed to "seeing differences" and when "everything [has] fallen into place in my mind, I will no longer see anything worthy of note, I will *no longer see* what I am looking at" (168).

At the same time, Calvino's interest in ancient civilizations implies a return to the origin if not of the galaxy, at least to that of humankind. At the root of all this we find the implicit, yet persistent desire to recover from within the past a suprahistorical human quintessence, a code of "primordial and atemporal instincts" (46). In the final essay collected in the volume, "*Le fiamme in fiamme*" Calvino tells of his visit to a temple located in central Iran. After contemplating the mihrab, an intricate door frame that faces Mecca but encloses a naked wall (and not as one would expect open space), he understands that the object (*il fine ultimo*) of the desire made manifest in the plastic and literary arts is ineffable:

> The idea of perfection that art pursues, the wisdom accumulated in writing, the dream of satisfying every desire that is expressed in the splendor of the ornaments, everything refers back to a single meaning, celebrates a single principle and foundation, implies a single object. And it is an object that is not there. Its only quality is its not-being-there. You cannot even give it a name. [210]

Calvino senses that to reach the object of desire—for him the transcendental signifier—is to comprehend the void of non-being, through the end of this temporal cycle and the passage from nonbeing back to nothingness.

Inside the temple where the sacred flame of the Parsi is kept alive, he listens to prayers recited in Avesta, the language "in which the most ancient stratifications of the Indo-European family of languages are preserved" (221). He asks himself if perhaps he has gone to the temple to hear "an echo of the mythic origins of spoken language" or perhaps to verify if this flame that has been kept alive for hundreds of years is somehow different from all others (221–22). "What am I looking for among the faithful of Ahura Mazda, the first deity to reveal itself to the Indo-Europeans as the supreme transcendental principal?" he asks (223). As he stares into the holy flame, the "mythic" origins of language and of human civilization blend in his mind with the fire that gave birth to the elements, the universe, the stars, and the earth. This sacred flame, he imagines, will burn until it becomes one with the fire of general conflagration and decomposition of the universe. The flame of the Parsi comes to symbolize for Calvino the alpha and the omega of both human civilization and matter.

What will happen, he then asks, when the supply of combustible material is exhausted? "Is it possible to conceive of a fire that has been kept alive since the beginning of time and will never be extinguished?" (225). His lengthy answer bears direct quotation, because in the fire he sees what he has been searching for all along, "the substance of the universe":

> The world I inhabit is governed by science, and this science has a tragic foundation: the irreversible process that leads the universe to decompose in an immense blaze. What will remain of all livable and visible worlds will be a fine dust made of completely indistinguishable parti-

cles. Near and far, before and after will be one huge blur. Here among the Ahura Mazda's faithful, in the fire that safeguards against the darkness, in the fire the *mobet* lulls and reawakens with his psalms, the substance of the universe is shown to me in the combustion of that which it mercilessly devours: the form of space as it expands and contracts, the rumbling and the crackling of time. Time is like fire: first it dashes forward in an impetuous flare, then it lurks hidden in the slow carbonization of the epochs, and then it twists and darts away in lighteninglike and unpredictable zigzags. But it always heads toward its only possible destination: the consumption of everything, including itself. When the last fire dies out, time too will end. Is this why the Zoroastrians keep their fires alive? The thing I think I am on the verge of understanding is this: to suffer because the arrow of time speeds toward a void makes no sense. Everything in the universe that we would like to save exists only because it is combustible. To exist means to be consumed. The only possible way to exist is like the flame. [225–26]

IV. Palomar

At first glance the narrative *tasselli* or *tesserae* of which *Palomar* is composed seem to be so many isolated events culled from a fictionalized autobiography (Tornabuoni). Their symmetrical arrangement within a three-dimensional field of Cartesian coordinates would belie an intellectual distress that must necessarily unfold diegetically, in a manner that reflects the progression of Palomar's thought, retracing a process of maturation and epistemological travail up through its culmination in defeat. The fragmentary nature of the narrative is resolved in a unifying center of gravity constituted by the narrating *I*, who tragically would embrace life at the very moment it abandons him.

At the heart of Palomar's inquiry are questions regarding the self and observation, and, to be more specific, the problematic nature of received modes of thinking. How does one, he asks, look at "the world from within an *I* that can (*possa*) dissolve and become pure observation?" (93).

His response is to deny or negate his own subjectivity by adopting a latter-day *chosisme* that he equates with "objectivity." In order to become "objective" or a "pure observer," he must devise for himself an investigative method or mode of observation. This problem is resolved when Palomar comes to the conclusion that "the key to mastering the complexity of the world" is synonymous with "reduc[ing] that complexity to the simplest of mechanisms" (14). Therefore, he will look at minimal units "objectively," and attempt to abstract a general theory through induction. Initially this process of abstraction coincides with an attempt to go beyond cultural constraints (something he so awkwardly tries to accomplish, for example, in "*Il seno nudo*") eschewing, paradoxically, objectifying social dialog. That is, he will not seek social verification of his observations but "concern himself only with what is seen" (44).

But how does one go beyond subjectivity and received modes of thinking to glimpse the essence of phenomena? A first important step for Calvino-Palomar, as we have seen, is the acknowledgment of a material world that exists autonomously of the subject, accomplished when he realizes "the moon no longer needs him" to exist (36).

When he asks which came first, the sun's rays or the eye that perceives them, he begins to understand and accept that an objective, material world exists independently of his observation of it:

> Mr. Palomar thinks about the world without him: the boundless world that preceded his birth and the even more obscure one to follow his death; he tries to imagine

> what the world was like before there were eyes, any eyes at all; and he tries to imagine a world that tomorrow due to catastrophe or slow corrosion were to become blind. What happens (happened, will happen) in the world? . . . He is convinced that the ray of light will exist after he is gone. [25]

Once a state of supreme detachment has been achieved, the next problem he addresses is how to observe (64). Palomar quickly resolves to utilize a phenomenological approach to the world and "limit himself to looking, fixing in the smallest detail, the little he is able to see, sticking to the unmediated ideas suggested to him by what he sees." But then Palomar asks himself what, within the visual image, is indicative of the essence of a specific phenomenon. If this can be ascertained, he might then begin to comprehend its specific internal harmony and then abstract from it a general theory of the many nonhomogeneous harmonies, the totalities within larger totalities evoked in "*L'aiola di sabbia*," that compose the cosmos.

This pursuit of harmonies is at the center of Part 2 and is carried forth in the hope of reaching the "final meaning" (*il senso ultimo*) of existence. Palomar "always hopes to uncover a pattern or a constant" (81) in all that he observes. His search for a cohesive essence or "harmony" and "the search for a means of escape from the uneasiness of living" (84) are one and the same. After reflecting on his own biography, Palomar retraces the bifurcations of evolution back toward "a first dawn of culture in the long biological night" and the origin of the species (84). However, he must stop far short of the "ineffable final meaning" (84) he seeks.

After contemplating the albino gorilla ("the only existing example of a form not chosen" [84]) he chances upon—in the concluding segment of Part 2—the squamata, a life form that predates anthropoids, living vestige of "the world that preexisted man, and of the one that will succeed him" (87). The reptiles are emblematic of a significant path not taken and of the apocalyptic vision that emanates from this text, specifically Palomar's repressed fear of death, his own and that of the species. Reptiles not only show "the human world is not eternal and is not the only one possible" (87) but more important, they are indicative of what for him at this point in time is "the only recognizable order in the world" (86): the classificatory schema of species, genera, and phyla by which the biological sciences construct an overview of animate life forms. Much like Dantès who "wrote" his prison, we create these taxonomies or intellectual paradigms and then are imprisoned by them when, as a necessary consequence, they determine our thought:

> Each specimen of this antediluvian bestiary is kept alive artificially, as if they were nothing more than intellectual hypotheses, products of the imagination, linguistic constructs, paradoxical argumentations whose only purpose is to demonstrate that the only possible world is our own. [87-88]

Viewing this prehuman world evokes in him images of the many cosmic and evolutionary paths not taken:

> Each window contains a sample of the worlds from which humanity is excluded, torn from a natural continuum that might never have existed. [87]

He would like to repress the thought that all human life could also have never come to be, but he is haunted by the immanence and ineluctability of nonbeing:

> In what time frame do they exist? In that of the species, outside the flow of time that rushes the individual from birth to death? Or do they experience time as geological epochs, following the rhythm of the shifting of continents

> and the hardening of the earth's crust? Or in the slow cooling of the sun's rays? He cannot bear the thought of a time frame outside our experience. Palomar can visit the reptile pavilion only occasionally and then he must hurry through. Once again he beats a hasty retreat. [88]

As Part 3 opens ("*L'aiola di sabbia*") a "silent" Palomar continues to believe his general theory will be excogitated "with the simplest of means and without recourse to concepts expressible in words" (91). He resolves to go beyond the relativity of the individual, join with the collective *I* postulated in Calvino's ekphrastic studies, and "contemplate the absolute." He would become a "pure" or "objective" observer, "an eye that registers facts and transmits them" (Nascimbeni). When suddenly he intuits "a possible harmony" of "nonhomogeneous harmonies," or concentric totalities, he thinks that perhaps the human can be reintegrated into the natural world after all. In the "*aiola di sabbia*" he notices:

> Between humanity-sand and world-crag one senses a possible harmony, as if between two nonhomogeneous harmonies: that of the nonhuman in an equilibrium of forces that does not correspond to any pattern and that of human structures which aspire to the rationality of a geometrical or musical composition, never definitive. [93]

In "*Il modello dei modelli*" Palomar contemplates the use of deductive reasoning to project the construction of a general theory whose point of departure is the inherited axioms that form the basis of our intellectual paradigm (104). One may begin with a system, he notes, and then verify it against empirical observations, adapting the system and the data to coincide with each other as research progresses. However, as he recapitulates his quick disenchantment with this method (105–6), the reader understands that

Palomar is recounting the shift in Calvino's intellectual biography from a youthful, utopian *progettualità* grounded in deductive reasoning to an inductive method whose point of departure is phenomenological defamiliarization and observation of the particular and whose intended point of arrival is a general theory of multiple totalities:[3]

> Now he needed a wide variety of models, reciprocally transformable, perhaps, so that they could be adapted to each other according to a combinatoric procedure. [106]

But as Calvino/Palomar retraces his intellectual autobiography, the reader has the presentiment of the imminent undoing of his epistemological project, of the definitive clash of the contradictions inherent in the underpinnings of his grand design. Palomar finds himself "face to face with a reality that can be mastered only with great difficulty and cannot by any means be made homogeneous" (106). Self and world appear to him as incommensurate totalities.

This progression culminates, and all of Calvino-Palomar's theories unravel, in the nonaction of the final section of the text, "*Le meditazioni di Palomar*" (3.3). In "*Il mondo guarda il mondo*" Palomar's attempts at objective observation are frustrated by the insistence of learned patterns of observation. "He quickly realizes that he is ruining everything, just as he always does when he involves his own ego and all the problems he has with his own ego" (109).

Palomar's phenomenological observation of objects excludes social intercourse with "other myselves." However, rather than look inside the self for an essence that might serve as the basis for dialog with others ("I have never felt," he admitted, "a strong urge to explore psychological interiorities" [Cds 33]), he concentrates on eliminating the self entirely from his considerations. But in order to go beyond subjectivity, he must imagine that what is under scrutiny does the looking; he must imagine the watched is watching him. To quote Palomar, "the trajectory that connects the watcher to the watched must initiate with what is watched" (109). In other words, he would see himself through the eye of another. But this process is predicated on his having first intuited the essence of what is watched. As Palomar muses:

> A thing is happy to be watched by other things only when it is convinced that it signifies itself and nothing else, among other things that signify themselves and nothing else. [110]

However, when "the world looks at the world" (3.3.1) he realizes that any proposal he might advance hinges on his own subjective perception. Now, having discarded a priori any form of social or dialogic objectification, he must choose. Either his subjective view of reality is to be imposed on others or—if pure observation is to be achieved—the subject must negate itself. But since he has already determined that the pure observer must by definition be bereft of subjectivity, it cannot be watched. Thus, his efforts at objective self-effacement, at reducing himself to a mere "mirror" in which the world sees itself reflected, are thwarted.

At this point the contradictions in his reasoning enter into a culminating phase of irreconcilable conflict. If, as Palomar believes, the macrocosm is reflected in its internal harmonies or microcosms, then he is justified in looking inward with the hope of finding within himself a systematic harmony that he can apply by analogy to both society and the universe. But when Palomar contemplates a world that looks at itself, it is a world of objects, not one of interiorities. At the same time, he is convinced that if he is to live in the world, he must learn to live with his fellow human beings. He concludes he must better his relationship with society before attempting to learn about the larger totality, the world of objects: "the idea that everything in the universe is interconnected and affects everything else never abandons him" (112). Moreover, he has already determined that the world of objects must be observed "objectively."

His theories come undone when he apprehends that nonsubjective communion with phenomena cannot be reconciled with necessarily subjective self-awareness and with mutual comprehension and interaction in the social realm:

> While contemplating the heavens he had grown accustomed to considering himself an anonymous and bodiless point; he had almost forgotten he existed. Now if he were to deal with human beings he could not avoid placing himself in the equation, but he no longer knew where his himself was. [113]

Ironically, placing himself in the equation is precisely what he has resisted most strenuously all along:

> The people he admired for their eloquence and nonchalance were first of all at peace with themselves, and then with the universe. Palomar did not love himself and so he had always done the utmost to avoid face-to-face encounters with himself. This is why he preferred refuge among the galaxies. Now he understands that he must begin by seeking out an interior peace. [113–14]

Palomar's quest for a general theory is frustrated once again by his inability to locate a point of origin for his thought. He falters between the world of objects, the social and the self, but the comprehension of each of these is contingent on the understanding of the other two elements of the equation.

Stymied, he reverts to a prior strategy, that of self-negation. He imagines going beyond cultural constraints and inherited modes of thinking and considers nonbeing: he "learns how to be dead":

> Now then, being dead is not as easy as you might think. First of all, you must not confuse being dead with nothingness, a condition that occupies the endless distance of time that precedes birth, apparently symmetrical to the equally unbounded time that follows death. In fact, before birth we are one of the infinite possibilities that may or may not come to be realized. Once dead, we can neither be realized in the past (to which we now entirely belong but can no longer affect) nor to the future (which, even though it has been affected by us, is forbidden to us). [115–16]

He sees death as his only means of overcoming subjectivity and of realigning himself with the larger totality. However, as soon as he sees death as the most "natural" of states, he is repulsed by it. Although Calvino would argue for the superiority of closed systems (Cds 50), such as death or nonbeing, the open-endedness of becoming is now revalued: the living can modify the meaning of their past through new actions. They can adjust and modify the "internal architecture" (118) of the system. A living author can change the meaning of the entire sequence by adding new "tarots" and reconfiguring those already on the table. Death, on the other hand, signifies foregoing agency and admitting that "one's life is a closed unity" (118), a fixed, inalterable *combinatoire*.

Death, then, is the shoal on which Palomar's epistemological project flounders. Palomar, as we have seen, is incapable or unwilling to engage in self-analysis. His lack of self-understanding prevents interaction, or transitivity, in the social realm. Since he cannot understand the self intrinsically or through comparison and contrast with the social, he contemplates what the self is not: the nothingness and nonbeing that precede and follow being. Nonbeing provides the individual with a definitive definition because it precludes ulterior growth and development. However, he comes to realize that if death (nonbeing) is to have meaning, it can only have meaning for others, those who survive and interpret the individual. In other words, there must be a future in death. However, nonbeing is of no import to the intransitive subject; thus, death "has no future" for Palomar. It can only acquire significance when a dialog takes place in absentia between posterity and the transitive subject Palomar refuses to be.

This diegetic progression culminates in the concluding *tassello*, "*Come imparare a essere morto*" (3.3.3), when the contradictions inherent in Palomar's epistemological and ontological project cause it to come undone. As he passively watches his enterprise unravel, he comes to understand the only avenue left open to him is that of complete self-negation (in his phrasing "sublime detachment" [117]) and death. Although both metaphorical (through abdication of authority over the text) and physical death are the logical consequence of the prospected move beyond subjectivity and agency, Palomar is suddenly overwhelmed by the immense and terrifying distance separating subject-author and posterity-reader. On one side of the gap is the "dead" author, in the Barthesian sense, who has consigned the text and can no longer alter the sequence of tarots and, as a result, the right to assign meaning to the narrative sequence. On the other are the living, those who create the text through reading and interpretation.

Palomar has consistently eschewed social transitivity or incisiveness. Therefore, one would expect that death would be welcome to him: he can definitively consign the task of ascribing a meaning to the text of his life to the reader and forego interaction with posterity. However, he is overtaken by the desire to continue living. Ego instincts of self-preservation overtake the death wish that informs the desire to be no more than an "eye suspended over the world." Now he would gainsay death by "dilating" and describing in infinite detail each instant of his life. Whereas he was once convinced that the "final meaning" of an individual's life was sealed by death, he now understands that death only prevents the individual from actively participating in the interpretation of his own life. Tragically, Palomar is made to abdicate control over his text at the very moment in which he wishes to assert his authority over it.

6 Postmodern Multiperspectivism

I. The Oppositional Postmodern Narratives of Morrison, Doctorow, and Tabucchi

The oppositional postmodern narratives of Morrison, Doctorow, and Tabucchi recuperate elements of past praxis that have been written out of historiographic recountings of the past. In their work, history (with a lower-case h) is represented not as a process of unilinear evolution, a concatenation of causes and effects culminating in the present. Rather, their microhistories include, as part of their dynamics, forgotten events whose latent presence are acknowledged as part of a constantly changing present. They purposely recover dialectical "fragments," placing them, to use Benjamin's term, in "meaningful juxtapositions," capable (because they redefine the present as an assemblage in continuous flux) of modifying the course of human behavior in the future.

In marked contradistinction to the Kunderian historical "lightness" sought out by the immanent narrator of Calvino's *Se una notte*—for whom the past was a "tapeworm" (106)—and to metafiction's leveling and transcendence of its own historical context, Morrison, Doctorow, and Tabucchi move beyond the isolation of high and late modernism and break out of the continuous present or compression of temporal horizons installed in postmodernity. Although the stylistic strategies of the postmodern narratives we will have occasion to cite differ greatly, they are associated by their willingness to brush history against the grain and give voice to the historically marginalized. Unlike esthetic or ludic narrative reactions to postmodernity, which ground themselves in metatextuality and self-irony, oppositional postmodernisms do not reduce all praxis to literary history. Instead, they recuperate and valorize in the present those untextualized traces of past reality that survive in conscious and unconscious memory and in orally transmitted knowledge.

Benjamin has written of the need to reenter into legibility latent traces of the past so that a new situational value, relative to the present, may be assigned to them. Oppositional postmodernism's restoration to the present of latent, disparate elements of the past subverts all strong, exclusionary historical narratives. Within the present there are traces of the silenced and marginalized "detritus of history," to use Benjamin's term. For Benjamin the present is a "constellation" of "dialectical images"—that is to say, the historicity of the present is the sum of the textualized past and its unwritten detritus. When the "dialectical images" of the forgotten past are displaced from their context and reinscribed into the present, they gain focus within the present and constitute its "potentially revolutionary antithesis."

In postmodernity, primarily because of the revolution in information technology, commonsense conceptions of time and space are radically modified. The geographic mobility of capital to displace investments intensifies the demographic movability of industrial societies. The forced transience of the work force strips the individual of any sense of place or tradition, severely restricting the weight of the past in decision-making.

The corollary of the diminished importance of the past is the shortening of future horizons. Decisions must now be made much more quickly than in the past if one is to keep pace with, for example, the rapidity of the electronic stock market tote board. In addition, the impending threats of planetary annihilation through nuclear holocaust and environmental destruction severely limit future expectations.

These changes condition how we conduct our daily lives. They are reinforced by the installation in video culture of a continuous present that does not enhance knowledge and understanding of the world, but presents current affairs in fragmented bits of episodic information. The antecedents and consequences of televised news are ignored, while the content of the information itself is mystified by the deliberate concealment of the ideology of the corporate sponsors who prop up the myriad talking heads animating our television screens. Moreover, as Jameson has written, our lives are no longer governed by the cycles of nature, but by the perpetual change of the fashions conjured up by media images. Our seasons are postnatural, artificial constructs of commercial convenience (*The Seeds of Time* 17–19).

The purposive recuperation of the past in oppositional postmodern narratives undermines and contests the continuous present of postmodernity by restoring an objectifying perspective that utilizes dialogic points of reference. Oppositional postmodern narratives assert that the present can be understood and made manageable only in light of a past comprised not only of dominant discourse but also of the counterdiscourses it tends to delegitimate. A perspective that embraces the past can look to the future and, more importantly, orient itself in the present. Moreover, when the subject sees itself being seen by what is other, the panoptic perspective of a polycentric reality is valorized. Temporal and objectifying points of orientation are utilized by oppositional postmodern narratives as guides through the maze of unattainable and unfounded relativistic "truths" that characterize postmodernity. When postmodern narratives move outward from the subject to acknowledge the interdependence of the self and the other, deprivileging and undermining the authorial voice through the multiplication of the narrative center, their narratives surmount the radical atomization and unifying perspective of high and late modernist literature. They work to reestablish social bonds and strengthen the temporal and spatial points of orientation debilitated by postmodernity.

Oppositional postmodern literature, then, becomes, as Benjamin proposed, the organon of history and its task that of giving voice to silent "remnants of the past." To this end, in *Beloved*, ever deeper, historical realities are gradually revealed, exposing the effects of the limiting case of slavery and of racism on the American national psyche. The novel is a very concrete example of how and why a strengthened temporal perspective can and must be used for guidance as we move toward the future.

Doctorow, in *The Waterworks*, exposes the inverted premises on which the specifically American "concordance of wealth, government, and science" are founded (*The Waterworks* 238). Doctorow argues that all our self-definitions are predetermined by dominant interpretations of the past. What is commonly referred to as history is in truth a reification or "myth." These self-styled definitive readings of the past come under interrogation in Doctorow's work so that the ideals on which the American republic were founded may once again be a factor in contemporary political debate. To recuperate the past in *L'angelo nero*, Tabucchi discombobulates the narrating self into multiple, heteronymic others. Through his surrealistic recovery of the repressed, he interrogates the social, political, and intellectual contexts that determined and condition to this day at least one generation of Italians.

II. Morrison: Reinscribing History in *Beloved*

A. *Village Values, Communal Narration, Reader Participation*

Toni Morrison spurns labels, such as black writer or woman writer, that would categorize her work, condition how it is read, and help with its merchandising. Behind Morrison's rejection of such facile designations is a desire to challenge racial, gender, and class boundaries, and transcend the racial specificity characteristic of her purposive recuperation of traits of African American narration.[1] In *Beloved*, slavery in the United States, certainly a most dramatic example of inhumanity, speaks eloquently to the ingrained racism that will mar and condition the American psyche far into the next millennium, to the ethnic hatreds that have again resurfaced in a Balkanized Europe, and to the myriad everyday violations of humanity that surround us—both those textualized in newspapers and police blotters and their "unspoken" counterparts, the repressed detritus of history.

Through the act of writing, Morrison puts herself in touch with a collective memory whose function is to focus the many discordant and quiescent, yet potentially meaningful, elements of the past that survive in the present (see *Black Women Writers at Work* 131). The overriding importance of the collective understanding of the past gives shape to what she calls "village" or community values. "Village values" provide the individual with a defining humus. Within the community the individual first discovers social purpose, regard for others, and an appreciation and understanding of collective experience ("City Limits, Village Values" 38). Subsequent to their appropriation, the community's values serve as locus of the individual's self-assertion when they are transcended and defied ("Memory, Creation, Writing" 389).

The community values that emanate from Morrison's writings are a source of "alternate wisdom" and psychological sustenance. The community serves Morrison's characters as point of orientation and of "symbolic placement,"[2] necessary for the resistance to and the defiance of the dominant socio-economic system ("City Limits, Village Values" 43).

Morrison perceives a lack of historical depth in the narratives of authors typically labeled postmodern and believes this tenuousness belies a "great rent" in the American psyche and spirit. In her view, the repression of history constitutes an attempt to distance oneself from the events in question and to fashion one's own personal innocence. At the same time, the individual's "struggle to forget" and elude the past are endemic to the dominant culture. In the United States, she has said, "the past is absent or it's romanticised. This culture doesn't encourage dwelling on, let alone coming to terms with, the truth about the past" ("Living Memory" 11).

In contrast to metafictional modernist writers, Morrison says she is "not interested in indulging [her]self in some private, closed exercise of [her] imagination that fulfills only the obligation of [her] personal dreams" ("Rootedness" 344). The social isolation that emanates from the more or less thinly veiled autobiography of contemporary writers who write about the act of writing is, in her opinion, "inimical" to those "characteristics of black artistic expression and influence" ("Rootedness" 339–40) that center on the interaction of the social group and its individual members. Thus, the fundamental relevance of the past compels Morrison to look far beyond the writerly self-sufficiency of metafiction toward a "sharable world." In a recent collection of essays she says that "the imagination that produces work which bears and invites rereadings, which motions to future readings as well as contemporary ones, implies a sharable world and an endlessly flexible language" (*Playing in the Dark* vii). "Flexible language" forestalls both authorial abdication from and control over the text. It also fosters dialogs among equals that affirm the validity and the interdependence of writerly and readerly recountings of a shared past. While theoreticians and practitioners of contemporary metafiction claim that the incorporation of metatextual references undermine both the text and what is inscribed within it, they are in the final analysis purely esthetic solutions that passively accept our condition of postmodernity. Oppositional postmodern narratives, on the other hand, resist postmodernity by attempting to know and transform the present.

Much contemporary postmodern narrative and theory give great purchase to the parody of the history of representation, claiming that it undermines univocal interpretations of the textualized past. However, just as John Barth's metafiction proves to be radically subject-centric, metatextual irony confines its field of reference to literary history (and its audience to those who have read the parodied work), validating itself through redundancy. As Morrison emphasizes, such irony does not multiply interpretive possibilities, rather it determines and limits future readings. Therefore, in her work she deliberately avoids metaliterary references that evoke an already established, self-authenticating literary world. In her view, recourse to the literary tradition ultimately impoverishes the reader's imagination and restricts the reader's ability to "work *with* the author in the construction of the book" ("Rootedness" 341).

Rather than condition future readings by providing a metatextual frame of reference, Morrison encourages reader participation by creating in her fictions aural "gaps," which are constituted primarily by the absence of adverbs. In other words, she wants each reader to ascertain individually whether the characters are speaking loudly, for example, or calmly or angrily. In addition, as she has specified, reader participation is stimulated when there are lacunae in what the immanent narrator can know and recount:

> Into these spaces should fall the ruminations of the reader and his or her invented or recollected or misunderstood knowingness. The reader as narrator asks the questions the commmunity asks, and both reader and "voice" stand among the crowd, within it, with the privileged intimacy and contact, but without any more privileged information than the crowd has. That egalitarianism . . . places us all (reader, the novel's population, the narrator's voice) on the same footing." [Unspeakable Things Unspoken" 29]

The reader is denied access to a viewpoint above the fray, a vantage that would be provided by an omniscient narrator. At the same time, when the reader joins the chorus an egalitarian dialog is established and additional layers of the palimpsest, those the individual reader, and not the author, deems most significant are placed in relief. Thus, previously erased remains of the past regain focus in the present.

The addition of the reader's voices to the chorus makes it seem as if the story has no author. This feeling of "effortless" aurality, of having "the reader *feel* the narrator without *identifying* that narrator" ("Rootedness" 341) is effected in great measure by the graceful transitions between the direct representation of conversation to the indirect discourse of memory. When the reader joins with the chorus, the story is modified by the new voices that contribute to it and comment on it, emphasizing certain aspects of the story over others (McKay 421).

Parenthetically, and as we have seen, for Calvino combinatoric retelling connoted the "apocryphal" rendition of foundational myths. Following Croce, Calvino stressed the centrality of the author who internalized what he heard. Morrison, on the other hand, attempts to create a narrative that, like folktales, "are told in such a way that whoever is listening is in it and can shape it" (Darling 6). For Benjamin the story, in contradistinction to the simple transferral of information, does not aim at transmitting the pure in-itself of the event, but embeds it in the life of the person reporting, in order to pass it on as experience to those listening.

Morrison avoids metaliterary references in order to place all readers on an equal intellectual footing: the ability of culturally privileged readers to more fully appreciate a work that uses metatextual citations is nullified. Contemporaneously, Morrison restores the articulateness of her illiterate characters and acknowledges in them an intellect commensurate to that of the reader. She does not attempt to depict the speech patterns of the ex-slaves who populate *Beloved* through the obtrusive presence of mimetic, nonstandard grammar ("a certain mode of language in which you just sort of drop g's" ["Rootedness" 342]). Rather, African American aurality is characterized through "manipulation of metaphor" (McKay 427), a tonality that consists principally in the anthropomorphization of nature and the characters' surroundings—nature is considered humanity's consociate in a manner that evokes the sacrality of all life—and in the deanthropomorphization of a violated humanity.[3] As a result, a non-assimilable diversity[4] is legitimated, and an eloquent and sonorous voice is given to the historically muted.

The importance of community values and of remembrance in Morrison's work is often stressed by both the author and her commentators. However, surpisingly little has been said about the stylistic novelty that choral narration brings to the text. The quasi-panoptic perspective of the communal narrator gives rise to a form of narration that is comprised of many different voices. Each of these voices contributes his or her limited understanding of events to the recomposition of the tale. In *Beloved* there is no reified osmosis of author and character, a trait of free indirect discourse. The characters' experiences are not superseded by, nor absorbed within, the author's point of view. Morrison also forswears the creation of an omniscient, third-person narrator who knows the thoughts of all the characters and would be thus empowered to editorialize, judge the characters, or reassure the reader. Instead, she artfully effects a hybrid of direct, yet nonmimetic discourse and an indirect *quasi*-omniscient depiction of the thoughts of the characters through what I refer to as a communal or choral narrator.

The communal narrator Morrison installs, because it brings together a plurality of voices, unavoidably lacks the innocent eye of the first-person narrator. Hence there is no discrepancy between what the immanent narrator and the reader know. Morrison's communal narrator is comprised of a chorus of voices who know much, but not all, about each other, and more importantly do not know as individuals all there is to know about themselves. As a result, there exist several highly significant lacunae in what the choral narrator can know and recount. Within these "gaps" are to be found the historical origins of the overdetermining thoughts that influence the behavior of Beloved, Sethe, and Denver. In other words, when inner, psychic reality overtakes the reality of the outside world, and the character is not capable of explaining his/her actions, the reader is both free and obliged to bring to light and interpret the roots of those actions.[5]

"Village values" and the traits of the African American narrative traditions Morrison reinvigorates—aurality, audience participation, and chorality—interweave and inform each other reciprocally. The communal nature of the narration makes possible and catalyzes reader participation when the determining past is relived not as an objective, leveling metanarrative, but as a vital element in the reader's present. By giving an articulate voice to the historically speechless, and by refamiliarizing what has been made alien, she reaffirms the existence and legitimacy of an alternative cognitive world that attributes equal validity to orally- and textually-transmitted knowledge.

B. *Beloved*

Beloved, because of her appearance—her new dress and shoes, her "flawless" skin (51), "soft new feet" (53) and "lineless palms" (243)—and "the African conviction regarding reincarnation" (Carabi 39), a belief that allows Baby Suggs to add her reminiscences to the tale from beyond the grave (135ff.), easily gives rise to credence that she is an apparition. Morrison herself has attributed to Beloved a supernatural quality that has been underwritten by most commentators (with the notable exception of Ferguson). When one examines the text closely, however, Beloved has very little of the supernatural about her.[6] Nonetheless, attention has effectively been diverted from the diegetic unfolding of what very coherently subtends and propels the plot, the interdependence of the present and past as they are revealed through a masterfully crafted network of individual dramas and psychlogical relationships.

In truth, Beloved has been radically dehumanized. The traumata inflicted on her as an infant and those of her adolescence (her bondage and deprivation of any and all human consortium) leave her psychologically maimed. When she first appears, Beloved carries with her the emotional scars that have remained latent since she watched her mother (or maternal surrogate—Beloved's recollection is not clear) leap into the Atlantic Ocean, abandoning Beloved to fate on the bridge of a slave ship. She bears also the physical scars left by a neck-chain on what is chillingly described as "the kootchy-kootchy-koo place under her chin" (239). Beloved's dissociation from the origins of her trauma—the abduction from her home, the separation from her mother, witnessing the suicide of the maternal figure, the events of middle passage, and the time spent literally as a love slave—have effectively alienated her from temporal experience and removed her to the "eternal present" (117) of her isolated, fragmented memories. In her words, "all of it is now it is always now" (210).

Although Beloved's past remains shrouded in mystery, Sethe "told Denver that she believed Beloved had been locked up by some whiteman for his own purposes, and never let out the door. That she must have escaped to a bridge or someplace and rinsed the rest out of her mind" (119). This conjecture is later substantiated by Stamp Paid:

> Was a girl locked up in the house with a whiteman over by Deer Creek. Found him dead last summmer and the girl gone. Maybe that's her. Folks say he had her in there since she was a pup. [235]

In any case, what Beloved has repressed is well beyond the reach of the choral narrator. Perhaps because of the compound traumata suffered by Beloved during her childhood and youth, she becomes extremely dependant on and attached to Sethe. Her ploy to get rid of Paul D may, at least in part, be attributable to her lack of the ego boundaries she would have formed in a post-Oedipal stage had she been afforded the chance to define herself in terms of her mother.

Since what we can glean of her past reveals no trace of any act of self-confirmation, her seduction of Paul D may also be due in part to an overriding need to be loved. Although she aggressively pursues Sethe's lover, she wants to be designated as a sexual object: not the lover but the beloved. Her copulation with Paul D may also be read as a manifestation of an unconscious compulsion to repeat or relive the traumatic experience undergone at the hands of the Caucasian "ghosts without skin" who "stuck their fingers" in her and "said beloved in the dark and bitch in the light" (241).

The consequences for Beloved of her estrangement from the community and her mother are incalculable. Emblematic of Beloved's isolation from a supportive social context and of her dissociation from the past is her "traumatized" English. Just as Sethe forgot the language spoken by her mother and Nan when she was sold to Sweet Home,[7] Beloved's native language was dislearned during captivity.[8] Her loss of the "ancestor" precludes access to the accumulated knowledge and defining humus of the "village."

The separation from her mother prevents Beloved from developing the individuated sense of the self that young girls develop in the post-Oedipal period. Moreover, her want of identity—dramatically understated in the text—is a result of her loss, during infancy, of her name. Not by chance, the only marginalized character in the book with a precise anagraphic identity is white, "Miss Amy Denver. Of Boston" (85). In contrast, Paul D not only carries through Reconstruction his former master's surname, Garner, but also the middle initial used to enumerate him and distinguish him from his half brothers. On the other hand, Denver's name, given to her by her mother, evokes the relative freedom of Ohio. Sethe bears the name of her African father. It is emblematic of the refusal of her mother to mentally capitulate to her capturers.[9] Baby Suggs' and Stamp Paid's resistance transpires in their rejection of the names imposed on them by dominant society. Beloved—and this is emblematic of her nearly complete psychological disorientation—does not know what a surname is (52). She has repressed or perhaps never learned the name of the one white man she knew (119), the one who sexually abused her and alienated from her body.[10] Beloved was not the name given to Sethe's young house guest at the time of the former's birth in Africa. That name was lost forever when she was stolen away. Tragically, "everybody knew what she was called, but nobody anywhere knew her name" (274).

Because Beloved is dissociated from her past—she has "disremember[ed] everything" (118)—she can have no future. Her fate parallels that of her namesake, the dead infant, who also is without a past and consequently without hope for a future (Carabi 38). Sethe's first-born daughter, who is never called by name, is also deprived of an identity. As Denver recalls, Beloved "was not her [sister's] given name, but the one Ma'am paid the stonecutter for" (208). In contrast, Sethe, whose childhood is almost equally scarred, can began to "think it up" after Paul D and Beloved arrive, and contemplate "some kind of a future" (273).

Morrison has spoken to the need felt by black women and given voice in *Beloved* "to love something bigger than yourself" while not "sabotaging" one's individuality (Darling 6). According to Naylor, Sethe "place[s] all of the value of her life in something outside herself" (Naylor and Morrison 584), her children. This does explain to some degree the paradox of why Sethe, in order to remove her "most beautiful thing" from harm's way, would have killed her children. This hypothesis, however, leaves unexplored the possibility that Sethe was at an unconscious level attempting to preserve the tremendous feeling of accomplishment and of self-realization gained when she "extract[ed] choice from choicelessness" ("Unspeakable Things Unspoken" 25), freed her children from slavery, and then successfully got her mother's milk to her baby. A tacit—and therefore, perhaps, even more cruel—aspect of slavery was that it deprived its victims of any sense of accomplishment. Prior to her escape, the only achievement permitted Sethe—because with no expense whatsoever it increased the owner's property—was procreation. Therefore, the flight north of the Ohio River was all the more significant for her:

> Covering the lower half of her face with her palms, she paused to consider again the size of the miracle; its flavor.
>
> "I did it. I got us all out. Without Halle too. Up till then it was the only thing I ever did on my own. Decided. And it came off right, like it was supposed to. We was here. Each and every one of my babies and me too. I birthed them and I got em out and it wasn't no accident. I did that. I had help, of course, lots of that, but still it was me doing it; me saying, *Go on*, and *Now*. Me having to lookout. Me using my own head." [161–62]

Her ability to create life when hers was not her own, having "enough milk for all" her children (100), getting it to them for the most part unaided and then to nourish what she had given life to (something denied Sethe's mother) blend together and give substance to "her most beautiful thing." As a consequence, given Sethe's belief that death would not prevent her from protecting "the life she made" (163), she prefers killing her children rather than to surrender to those who might sully them (a fate commonly—and justifiably—regarded as worse than death [see 251]) and vitiate all she had achieved. Sethe initially considers Beloved no more than a "sickly, shallow-minded boarder" (62), "Denver's friend" (173). Only after Paul D moves out, depriving Sethe of the dialogic partner who helps revivify latent memories, does Beloved assume in Sethe's mind the guise of her reincarnated dead baby, a projection of the mother and "daughter [she] wanted to be" (203). Sethe, through Beloved, overcompensates for having killed her offspring, and atones for the guilt she feels for having irrevocably changed the quality of life of her own surrogate mother, Baby Suggs (89–90, 184).

Therefore, much attention has justifiably been given to the surrogate mother-daughter relationship between Sethe and Beloved. However, the pivotal figure of Denver, and the interaction and interdependence between her and her mother, has been widely ignored. It is commonly believed that Denver is slow-witted. However, Lady Jones, her former instructor, knew that Denver was in fact quite intelligent (247). Furthermore, Denver is depicted by Sethe as over dependent on her mother (11), "obedient and reliable" (99), yet "irritable and lonely" (62). What matters more is that Denver, according to her mother, is "self-manipulated" (99); that is to say, susceptible to the overriding influence of her own thoughts. Denver's loneliness and self-manipulation combine to "haunt" the house. Her "imagination produced its own hunger and its own food, which she badly need because loneliness wore her out" (28–29).

The arrival of Paul D causes Denver to feel "hot and shy" (12). Upon learning that Paul D knew her father, Halle, she almost overcomes her initial reaction and has to "fight an urge to realign her affection" for what becomes a potential paternal figure (13). However, when she senses she is being left out of the reminiscences of the two ex-slaves, her bashfulness is overtaken by loneliness (13). Denver "hates" worlds that exclude her (62), but that exclusion is to a great extent self-imposed. In any event, her isolation severely stunts the development of her adult personality.[11] Her resentment for what she perceives as her exclusion from the recollection of Sweet Home prompts Denver to "long, downright *long* for a sign of spite from the baby ghost" (12), which is quick in coming. After Denver (a large woman, she is described as "twice Beloved's size"

[74 and also 185]), retreats to an adjacent room, the house's pitching floors (43) "inexplicably" begin to quake and the sideboard jumps forward, much to the young woman's glee.

Denver's memories of the attempt Sethe made on her children's lives hinders post-Oedipal identification with the mother. Denver nurtures phantasies of the baby ghost, her "secret company until Paul D came" (205), and of her father's return. In her mind:

> [He] was coming and it was a secret. I spent all of my outside self loving Ma'am so she wouldn't kill me, loving her even when she braided my hair at night." [207]

Denver's brothers would terrorize the little girl with "die—witch!" stories about their mother, including instructions on how to kill Sethe, should the urge to murder her offspring ever possess their mother again. The weak mother-daughter bond (after her brothers run away, Denver reacts to the death of Baby Suggs with anger for having been left alone to fend for herself with Sethe [4]) results in the daughter's constructing an idealized image of the father she never knew ("My daddy was an angel man" [208]) and a family composed of her, the reincarnated sister, and Halle:

> We should all be together. Me, him and Beloved. Ma'am could stay or go off with Paul D if she wanted to. Unless Daddy wanted her himself, but I don't think he would now, since she let Paul D in her bed. [209]

Lost in the past is the extent to which the baby ghost is Denver's creation. We never learn who assailed the family dog (12) nor do we learn why Here Boy runs off when Beloved appears. We do know that only Denver correctly predicts that the dog will not return until Beloved departs (55). In fact, Denver is alway close to, but never identifiable with, the uncanny actions perpertrated by the baby ghost. The repressed memory of Sethe's violence against her own children, once restored to consciousness, becomes an ever-present fear of her mother that is in turn sublimated in the baby ghost (who, according to Denver—and very much like Denver—feels "lonely and rebuked" [13]) and holds "for her all the anger, love, and fear she didn't know what to do with" (103).

When a schoolmate asks her of Sethe's incarceration, memories of the days she spent with her mother in jail return to consciousness. The overpowering desire not to hear about that part of her past provokes a hysterical deafness that both truncates her only adolescent attempt at achieving personal autonomy and effectively segregates her from her surroundings for two years. During that time, Denver recalls:

> All I could hear was my own breathing and one other who knocked over the milk jug while it was sitting on the table. Nobody near it. Ma'am whipped Buglar but he didn't touch it. Then it messed up all the ironed clothes and put its hands in the cake. *Look like I was the only one who knew right away who it was*. [208, my emphasis]

Before and after her deafness (inexplicably cured when the baby stamps her feet in Denver's immediate vicinity [103]), the baby's anger "wore her out" (13, 103); nonetheless, she enjoyed knowing "the downright pleasure of enchantment, of not suspecting, but *knowing* the things behind things" (37). Only a paternal figure, Paul D, with a violent response and a "loud male voice" (37) will succeed in scaring away "the only company [Denver] ever had" (19), the "baby ghost" who calmed Denver's "unrestricted ... need to love another" (104).[12] Traumatized by the attempt on her life, the adolescent Denver unconsciously inflicts spiteful acts on an ego boundary she and her mother share—the house. At the end of the novel her unattended scars remain. Nonetheless, she can work through what disturbs her when the roles of mother and daughter are reversed and she can act positively on impressions passively received during infancy and childhood. Denver acquires "a self to look out for and preserve" (252) only when she is forced to take the initiative and care for Sethe.

The past and the individual character's reactions to it are at the center of *Beloved*. While Beloved's repression of the past is involuntary, Sethe has spent almost the last two decades fighting her "rebellious brain" (70), trying to forget her years as a slave at Sweet Home and those following her escape to Ohio. The past, for both Sethe and her neighbor Ella, was something to "stomp out" (236). Only when Paul D appears, her story becomes "bearable," something she can share dialogically, and "tell, refine, and tell again" (99). When Sethe attempts to recuperate the past, she can at last begin to hope in a future founded on "trust and rememory" (99). Paul D's departure deprives her of the external point of reference she needs to recuperate and manage the past. She is overwhelmed by inner psychic reality and, like Denver, makes Beloved the reincarnation of the child she slayed eighteen years earlier.

Sethe's literal and figurative retreat from the outside world into her home and mind is a flight from the past into what Sethe believes is the safe haven of a "timeless present" (184). "Giddy" from her second flight to freedom ([183, 191], the freedom of "no longer ha[ving] to remember" [183]), she "hurr[ies] time along [from Sawyer's restaurant] to the no-time waiting for her" at home (191). Through such contrast, the temporal sequence, and the individual's conscious and active participation in it, is posited in *Beloved* as the only possible locus of freedom.

Tragically, Sethe risked her life to escape from "Sweet Home where time didn't pass" ([243] and believes her daughter has returned to her from "the timeless place" [182]) only to find herself and her "daughter" "wrapped in a timeless present" (184). When Paul D "put[s] his story next to hers" (273), he helps restore a temporal dimension to her mental life, unearthing voiceless relics of the past. Just as

Sethe is then empowered to deal with the contradictions inherent in her present, the reader is obliged to confront the collective legacy of the past. The recurrence of the historically repressed shatters all blissful illusions of an innocent future and an objectifiable, shared reality is installed as point of orientation and reference.

Morrison has spoken of a "national amnesia" that has driven the memory of slavery from the national consciousness (Angelo 120). In *Beloved* she examines this misremembrance, with particular concern for its effects within and on the African American community. She acknowledges the psychological need of African Americans to put slavery behind them and to move from bondage to true social and economic freedom. However, she is also well aware of the collective need to analyze what has been repressed (see Darling 6). Beloved embodies all the ills of slavery and, in point of fact, reminds Paul D of something he is "supposed to remember" (234) but has effectively put out of his mind. Those who should most readily feel compassion for her, Sethe's neighbors—themselves former slaves—demonize her instead.

Moreover, Sethe and Denver—after Beloved's presence has forced them to deal with with all their cicatrized pyschological wounds—are heavily in her debt, yet they allow her to run away unhindered. The two women quickly rinse her from their minds and memory of Beloved soon fades away, because "this is not a story to pass on" (275). However, while the deliberate ambiguity of this closing refrain underscores the desire to forget, it is also, in Morrison's words: "a warning" (Carabi 88). It is certainly easier to repress and deny the past, to *pass* on Beloved's story, but for Morrison and her readerly chorus, it is a story to pass *on*.

III. Doctorow: Recuperating Parallel Images of the Past

Like Morrison, Doctorow believes that narrative serves as a bond between the individual and the surrounding community. Modernism, he has argued, has made us think of writing as an act of ultimate individualism when, in fact, writers are witnesses to the times in which they live. In his view, the modernist novel has abstained from acting "as a major and transforming act of the culture" and has instead confined itself to the author's experience. When it directs its attention exclusively to the problems of "the neurotic individual identity" ("Living in the House of Fiction" 460) it fails to address the concerns of its audience.

Because of the isolation and the unwillingness of the "psychologized ego," as Doctorow calls it, of high modernism and its self-reflexive metafictional counterpart to move outward and speak to the broader issues facing their contemporaries, the modernist novel has suffered a "loss of consequence" or of social relevance. In his words, "there is a timidity to serious fiction now, some modesty of conception and language . . . a disposition to accept some rule largely hidden, to circumscribe our analysis and our geography, to come indoors and lock the door and pull the shades and dwell in some sort of unresounding private life" (*Jack London* 111).

Therefore, not only is Doctorow attentive to the accessibility of his work to the nonprofessional reader ("Creators on Creating" 44), but, and this matters more, in his prose he works to breach the barrier modernism has erected between the fate of the individual and that of the collectivity (Trenner 50). Thus, of paramount importance for Doctorow is the ability of the novelist to interact with the world and to reaffirm "the central place of the sustained narrative critique in the national argument" (*Jack London* 114).

For Doctorow, "the moral immensity of the single soul" is cast in relief only when society at large is its antagonist (*Jack London* 112). The pathos inherent in fictive prose must be used by the writer to first engage and then educate the reader in a manner that avoids facile edification. In other words, the "private" world of the narrator must transcend the individual and evoke an ideal shared by the collectivity

(*Jack London* 152). In his work Doctorow utilizes the past to comment on concerns facing the larger community in the present. In other words, when the reader can identify with the historical world of the collectivity, which the writer reintroduces into the present, an "instructive emotion is generated in the reader from the illusion of suffering an experience not his own" (*Jack London* 151). At this point the "private" world of the individual ceases to be an idiosyncratic, incommunicable, "hermetic" world, as is the case with modernist literature and becomes an integral part of a sharable one.

Following Benjamin, Doctorow claims that the authority to narrate derives from the relevance of the story to the listener. If the counsel offered by the tale is of value—that is, if it addresses anxieties that beset both reader and narrator—then the story can be said to be realistic or true, even if what is recounted did not transpire in deed (*Jack London* 154). If the reader identifies with the pathos of the narrative, the result will be an enhanced understanding of both the object of narration and of the self. In turn the desires (and, as a consequence, behavior in the future) of the reader will be modified. In his words, "the imagination obviously imposes itself on the world, composes a world, which, in turn, affects what is imagined" ("A Spirit of Transgression" 42). Hayden White has argued that historiography "emplots" human drama in the past. That is to say, recounted events are reordered in a hierarchical structure of relationships and single events, when subsumed within an integrative whole, are endowed with meaning (*The Content of the Form* 9). Catalyzing and propelling this plot are conflicts between the desires of individual subjects and society's laws and mores. At the same time, in White's view, all narratives are informed by the moral awareness of the narrator who, through the act of storytelling, mediates this struggle between individual and community. To borrow his phrasing:

> Even if history attests to the fact that all men everywhere have always desired liberation from their condition as

> merely *social* beings, it also attests to the fact that they have never been able to satisfy that desire. Neither any practice actually established anywhere in history nor any science could ever direct us to what we *ought* to desire. ["Getting Out of History" 3]

Literature, then, is both a document of present desire and a force that modifies desire in the future: what we are and what we have the potential to become. According to Doctorow, the ideal or future desire evoked in fictive prose belongs to the "esthetic realm" and therefore need not be expressed in what he calls "realistic" language, which, to his mind, reflects the empirical, pragmatic knowledge we, as a society, utilize for our own economic well-being and self-interest at the expense of our moral sensitivity ("Ragtime Revisited" 43). In opposition to this "regime" of man-made, hence "infinitely violable facts" he proposes a "fictive use of language" that is grounded in sentiment and morality and coincides quite unpragmatically with what we know to be true and just (*Jack London* 153).[13] Unlike the "realistic" language of nonfiction, fictive language casts aside objectivity by reducing the "narrative distance" between writer and character ("Ragtime Revisited" 5). This can occur only when the writer identifies with the personal and historical situation of an-other and then uses language in a way that enables the individual reader to identify with the pathos inherent in the narrative.

The question of reader interpretations of his work is at most a specious one for Doctorow. What interests him is the witness the writer bears to the tensions created when human emotions confront material necessity and what is to be learned when the reader is allowed to participate in another's experience in a "morally illuminating" way (*Jack London* 111).

More germane for Doctorow than the question of narrative authority is the interrogation of the traditional distinction between fiction and nonfiction. Creative and factual prose, he reminds us, both contain an imaginative component. As for the purported objectivity of nonfictions, Doctorow points out that journalists are "writers of fiction who do not acknowledge that [they are] making things up" ("Ragtime Revisited" 4): they do not represent objective reality in its totality but instead creatively decide "what to look at and write about . . . what will exist and what won't exist" ("A Spirit of Transgression" 43). Historians also exclude facts irrelevant to or not supportive of their thesis as they reconstruct the past according to a highly personal view of what they believe "really happened."

Parenthetically, the immanent narrator of *The Waterworks*, McIlvaine, repeatedly admits to using such narrative techniques in constructing his historical account. Moreover, and to close the parentheses, neither journalistic nor historiographical narratives make any pretense of faithfulness to the chronology of the past. Rather, events are rearranged so as to construct a new order of signification. Therefore, Doctorow sees little difference between fiction and nonfiction. He feels completely justified in culling from the documentable past images or concepts he can reorganize in his fictions according to the needs of the present. He reconfigures the real and the "possibly real," historically verifiable fact and its imaginative evocation in "experience," to use Doctorow's term, or "remembrance," to borrow Benjamin's.

As we have seen, Doctorow argues that historical truths emanate from a "nonfactual witness which doesn't destroy the facts or lie about them or change them, but in some peculiar way illuminates them" ("Ragtime Revisited" 8). In other words, for Doctorow—as is the case with Benjamin—the past is not linked to the present by a deterministic chain of cause and effect. In his fictions images from the past are dialectically recuperated into the present. The truth value of such "nonfactual illumination" invalidates any claim the nonfictional narratives of historiography and journalism may make on the truth; historiography and journalism are not the exclusive arbiters of what really happened in the past. Furthermore, once a "nonfactual" narrative is told, it becomes part of the realm of the real, which is to say, remembered experience of the past. As he told an interviewer, "I'm under the illusion that all of my inventions are quite true. For instance, in *Ragtime*, I'm satisfied that everything I made up about [J.P.] Morgan and [Henry] Ford is true, whether it happened or not. Perhaps truer because it didn't happen" ("The Writer as Independent Witness" 69).

At the same time—and while fictive prose may justifiably be considered one truth among many—the acknowledgment of its subjectivity underscores its need of external legitimation, lest it suffer the same loss of consequence that has befallen modernist narrative. The only means of reconstructing an objectifiable vision of the past, and of textualizing the present, is through what Doctorow alternately calls a "multiplicity of witness" and a "democracy of perception." Since truth is not necessarily grounded in documentable fact, but is predicated on the acquisition of a panoptic perspective composed of many truths, a multiplicity of witness safeguards against any excessively strong, exclusionary reading of the past: the univocal truth that suffocates all others and quickly transmogrifies into reified myth.[14]

The quest for "truth," is a twofold process. First it is the "moving outward" from one's own subjective truth, toward a reintegration of the self into a social fabric woven from multiple voices. Second, it is the dialectical restoration within one's own narrative of voices that have been silenced by the reified or "mythical" truths promulgated by the dominant classes ("Fiction is a System of Knowledge" 456). When specific chapters of the past are dialectically juxtaposed to the present, the silenced or repressed truths of others may be reinscribed in the present. The juxtaposition of the traces of a revalorized past and the present undermines a conception of history as a causal concatenation of events and proposes an alternative view of the historical dialectic.[15]

Doctorow's conceptualization of past and present as parallel blocks of time distinguishes him from writers generally considered to be postmoderns but whose works are in point of fact examples of a radical or late modernism, such as Umberto Eco. Doctorow believes that we cannot deal with "the past as if it were preparatory to our own time" (*Jack London* 141; see also *The Waterworks* 11). In *The Waterworks* historically verifiable figures and events underscore the analogy Docotorow draws between the events in question (which are said to take place in 1871) and the period in which Doctorow wrote his novel, the 1980s. The representation and reconfiguration of the past (which, like the present, has as its immediate antecedents the assassination of a popular president and a war that turned the nation against itself) authenticate the narrator's depiction of a "conspicuously self-satisfied class of new wealth and weak intellect . . . all aglitter in a setting of mass misery" (12). It proposes to enable readers to better understand the times in which they live—in the case of *The Waterworks*, the Reagan years.

In contrast, in the "Postscript" to the *Il nome della rosa* Umberto Eco claims that a function of historical narrative is to "further clarify what happened in the past, and the significance for us of what happened" (519). In Eco's opinion, even though texts are subject to multiple interpretations, the reader can experience the "metaphysical thrill" (524) derived from uncovering the unequivocal source of the original impetus of the narrative: the unifying consciousness of the narrator. Eco's call for an "open work," to be molded through the cooperation of a writer and a "model reader," conceals but does not debilitate the strong, predetermining center constituted by his narrator. In fact, although the world Eco describes in *Il nome della rosa* can never be definitively structured, it is nonetheless—in Eco's words—a "structurable" world (524) linked by cause and effect to our own. For Doctorow the past is structured according the present's need to create a past in its own image, an image that reflects the present's evolving self-illusions: as the needs of the present change, so do its images of the past. Doctorow also insists that while the past can and should be used to explain the present, it must also catalyze self-analysis. The reconfiguring of the past must be an active part of a process of self-interrogation and not passive acceptance of collective self-illusions. For this reason Doctorow re-creates a historical past, which induces the reader to ponder what Americans might have become as a people had we not developed according to the dictates of individual and collective economic self-interest.

In his most recent book, *The Waterworks*, Doctorow purposely undermines the credibility of his first-person account of the history of New York City in the years subsequent to the Civil War. McIvaine's world is supposedly the objective one of events he transforms "into an object of language" (201). What little we know about his internal life and personal affairs seems irrelevant to the matter at hand. For example, his union-busting activities are mentioned in passing, as an inconsequential incident in his daily life (63). However, and in point of fact, this event does much to define McIlvaine as an organic member of the dominant classes. As we shall see, knowledge of McIlvaine's class of origin will implicitly clarify why he is struck dumb when his investigations lead him to "the truth."

McIlvaine recounts happenings he, for the most part, did not witness and did not report until decades later. Thus, undermining the credibility of the tale is, first, the imprecision inherent in the transferral of testimony from the witness to the recorder-reporter. Second, there is the tenuous reliability of memory (of both witness and reporter), which in this case is made increasingly suspect by the elderly narrator's admittedly waning lucidity (see 59 and 235). The narrator's lack of omniscience, underscored by the lacunae in what his sources tell him, further discredits the reliability and objectivity of what he has to say. Moreover, while placing a premium on the objectivity of his account, he paradoxically undermines the truth value of his own discourse when he informs the reader that the news he reports is something "construed" (14) and invented (28) by journalists who reorder the succession of events in order to bestow a determinate meaning on them.

In addition, McIlvaine's search for "the truth" and his attempt to convey what "really happened" is undermined in its very premises. In other words, as his investigation proceeds he unsuccessfully confronts a fundamental epistemological question—how do we know?—raised by his encounters with alternative, conflicting cognitive methods. On a more superficial level, the plot portrays the struggle for intellectual dominance between the faith of the Reverend Dr. Grimshaw and the enlightened, encyclopedic knowledge of the captain of police, Donne, on the one hand and, on the other, the positivism of the natural scientist, Dr. Sartorius. Their disagreement flares into a holy war between their traditional, spiritual morality and the amoral, "objective" science personified by Sartorius.

Sartorius's plan to create a breed of immortal posthuman cyborgs contrasts with "Christian society's" (238) belief in the immortality of the soul. This difference of opinion diverts attention from a third means of attaining eternal life to which Sartorius and Grimshaw, each in his own way, pay homage, participation in the supra-historical time of coinage. Nonetheless, when Sartorius proposes "recomposing" the Judeo-Christian God to reflect his view of humanity, he comes into conflict with those who profess that humanity was created in God's image. The strife comes to an end when Donne "restore[s] the proportions of things (191) by quashing what society believes is its "evil obverse" but is in fact a parody of its own metaphysical inversion or creation of a God who is a projection of its self-image. That is to say, both Sartorius and Grimshaw compose a God according to what each believes is humanity's image; their clash is merely between divergent, idiosyncratic views of humanity. For his part, Donne effectively transforms the "chaos and bewilderment" brought on by Sartorius's interrogation of common sense into something understandable by utilizing the power of the state to "recompose the world, comfortably in categories of good and evil" (140–41).

His interrogation of commonly held conceptions of society's self-image makes Sartorius a threat to it. Furthermore, by unmasking the general "servitude to wealth" (225) of all involved, he comes to represent a true danger to "Christian society," and his radically consequential logic undermines the self-illusions on which it is founded. To clarify: tacitly accepted by McIlvaine are the "sympathies for the moneyed class" harbored by "churchmen" and politicians. He chafes, however, when Sartorius explains to him the scientist's dependence on funding, perhaps because it reminds him of his own need of a publisher. This condition is shared by the artist who depicts "the faces and figures" of those who can afford immortality through portraiture (249).

Donne is well aware that Sartorius broke no law, but also knows that such "abnormal" or "insanely excessive" (230) argumentation cannot be tolerated. The latter's thoughts are dangerous not so much because they transgress social norms but because they expose and magnify contradictions masked by those norms. Therefore, Sartorius is sacrificed in a sort of morality play (236) that allows the public to believe that justice has been served even while the constitutional rights and ideals on which the country was founded are trampled. The subjugation of civil society to the whims of big money goes unquestioned and society heals itself by institutionalizing Sartorius.

Subtending this plot is another, more crucial epistemological conflict, which overshadows the false dilemma of traditional morality vs. amoral science: specifically, the confrontation of the positivist ways of knowing of Grimshaw, Donne, and Sartorius, on the one hand and, on the other, McIlvaine's modernist identification of reality and text. Although Grimshaw denounces "pagan" natural science from his pulpit, he uses the empirical methods of archeology to confirm "what faith already knows" and vitiate philological exegeses of sacred texts. Centuries of interpretations, to his mind, have reduced Scripture to a palimpsest of interpretations and reinterpretations. For this reason Grimshaw rails against his true enemy, which is not "pagan science" but the usurper of divine revelation, "the Redactor."

In contradistinction, for McIlvaine, editor par excellence,[16] the text is self-authenticating, not in need of physical validation. If something is written, it is real. In fact, no material evidence whatsoever substantiates his tale. Its veracity is contingent on his belief that the Waterworks once existed even though the structure survives only in texts, having long since been razed. Therefore, praxis is of no consequence to him. Events enter into reality only after they have been reported in the morning edition of his newspaper. This is why McIlvaine hails the balance sheet of the Tweed Ring as a divine revelation in its own right (149).

At the same time, "diction," or the right to textualize, for McIlvaine is synonymous with empowerment. Since, in his opinion, objectivity is "a way of constructing an opinion for your reader without letting him know that you are" (30), his charge as reporter is nothing less than "mak[ing] the collective story of us all" (11), of creating a signifying order out of chaos (14). Such "diction," or power, must be safeguarded against all encroachments so that the subjective truth of the pure, passive observer, the reporter, can hold sway. Paradoxically, the truth value or objectivity of what the reporter has to say, in his estimation, is contingent on a radical subjectivity that refuses to become a protagonist by "trespass[ing] . . . into the realm of cause and effect" (207)—thereby safeguarding another founding myth, that of the autonomous press (see 207).

Both the democratic ideals and self-illusory myths inherent in the American dream are embodied in the self-made man, Augustus Pemberton. Pemberton is a "captain of industry" with, according to Grimshaw, forgivable "Christian . . . imperfections" (139) which Pemberton carries to their extreme, logical consequences. However, just as the line of demarcation between "captain of industry" and "robber baron" is very tenuous, so is the one Grimshaw traces between "Christian imperfection" and "paganism." While Pemberton's sentiments "parody the normal person's" (222), he does not contradict "normality." His behavior in fact represents a limiting case of the contradictory means invoked by "Christian society" for achieving immortality: soul and capital.

His and Tweed's "paganism," then, are not considered the "evil obverse" of those imperfections, but merely their grotesque magnification. Tweed uses a combination of corruption and coercion to expropriate the state and subjugate the elaborators of its ideological superstructure. His identification with, or better, his expropriation of the state, both its ideological superstructure and economic base, is underscored by Donne's inability to injoin against him and by McIlvaine's dismissal from the newspaper (173, 175). Tweed's hybrid of legal and illegal capitalism surpasses Pemberton's only in its scope and magnitude. Contemporaneously, and this matters much more, it transcends all distinctions between legality and illegality on the one hand and, on the other, moral categories such as good and evil, a state of affairs that justifies his proclaiming himself "god of this city" (245). Pemberton and Tweed contribute to the constitution of a founding mafia of WASP bankers and industrialists that predate and determined the modus operandi of later ethnic manifestations of organized criminality.

Not only do Pemberton and Tweed blur all distinctions between legal and illegal ventures, but by identifying themselves with the state they commandeer its coercive police power. Moreover, their wealth affords them a position of dominance over their unwitting servants, those representatives of civil society who define and construct society's ideology. Having perverted "the American ideal" (31) through the establishment of an economic nobility, they need not choose between life and death, nor between heaven and hell, because they can buy into the "obverse Eden" (188) technology has built for them within their "inverted temple building" (60), the Reservoir.

McIlvaine is struck dumb when he stumbles upon the story he "secretly coveted . . . the writing of which might transcend reporting" (113), or the mere chronicling of events. He falls silent when he unwittingly unmasks all false ideals and self-illusions and understands that the various ways of knowing with which he is familiar, the intuition of the artist, religious faith, the encyclopedic knowledge of Donne, positivist science are merely pawns in the service of amoral, atemporal capital. Towering above his quest for "the truth" is a greater, concealed truth that takes shape in his ingenuous eyes as a conspiracy that surpasses the mere "concordance of wealth, and government, and science." It "left [his] eyes blasted to peer into it" (238) and McIlvaine unable to report it. The Ring is not a perversion of laissez faire capitalism but a grotesque magnification of its essence:

> The Ring, with their vaulting ambition, would carry ambition to its ultimate form. They were nothing if not absurd—ridiculous, simpleminded, stupid, self-aggrandizing. And murderous. All the qualities of men who prevail in our Republic. [192]

McIlvaine makes no attempt to hide his desire to possess this story. He covets the power of the journalistic exclusive to inform the historization of events. This is especially important to McIlvaine because of the extent to which he identifies with his text. As he says near the outset, "my life is wholly woven into the intentions of the narration, with not a thread remaining for whatever other uses I might have found for it" (64; see also 236).

Having identified with the narration, McIlvaine's subjective truth presumes to preclude and supplant any alternative, objectifying narration of these events. His unifying reality would ironically come to constitute a strong narrative center that subordinates all other "dictions" to his own. I say *ironically* because the objectification or validation he lacks—something that can be provided only by alternative perpectives—is exactly what leads McIlvaine to suspect that his tale is little more than the ruminations of a madman (235). His "exclusive," is merely an uncorroborated text (Sartorius's notebooks are either sequestered or destroyed [233] and no public record was made of the proceedings against him [236]). Nothing else exists to unify the narrative of "the only Author of the only Book" (145) on the Waterworks.

IV. Tabucchi: The Angel of History

A. The Self as Other

As is the case with Morrison, Tabucchi believes that a request for reader collaboration inheres in the act of writing. In his opinion, all writers—some knowingly, others not—ask their readers to make explicit everything the author either ignores, omits, or leaves unresolved. An example of such programmed "complicity of text and reader" (Costanzo), is Tabucchi's abstention from personally translating his oneirically autobiographical *Requiem*, written in Portuguese, into the Italian. As he explains, the alloglot distancing of the author positions the text as an unattainable point of arrival, thus safeguarding the "mysterious sense"—or Benjaminian aura—of the original ("Some Reflections on Translation"[17]). That is to say, since the mediation of the translator unavoidably forestalls direct communication between author and reader, concern for what the author wishes to convey cannot be predominant. The reader is thus freed to give vent to associations, "at home in the *mémoire involontaire*," that "cluster around the text" (Benjamin, *Illuminations* 186).

This, of course, does not completely explain why Tabucchi chose not to compose the original in his mother tongue. As an initial response, he claims that writing in a second language helps bring to the fore aspects of one's own personality that are not part of the conscious ego, but are hidden by what he calls the "hegemonic *I*." Acceptance of his own "linguistic schizophrenia" ("Some Reflections on Translation" 8) allows him to "escape from the constriction of [being him]self" (Borsari 7) and to explore the others usually concealed by and within a no longer monolithic ego. This method of self-analysis reveals an internally plural *I* whose different aspects, he insists, must not be reconciled or homologated, but accepted in their diversity ("Some Reflections on Translation" 10).

The disarticulation of the self and the consequent theorization of multiple subjectivities are the core of Tabucchi's poetic enquiry. Moreover, they demonstrate the central importance of the discovery of the Portuguese poet Fernando Pessoa's heteronymic theory for Tabucchi's work. Pessoa penned essays and verse using a plurality of signatures that, it must be stressed, were not pseudonyms. As Tabucchi explains:

> [Pessoa's heteronyms] are five poet-characters invented down to the most minute detail: each has his own biography, somatic features, aesthetic preferences, cultural background, and even his own idiosyncracies. Each lives, thinks, and composes verse with complete autonomy. [*La parola interdetta* 35–36]

"These five poets (six if you count the hortonym)," he adds, "all express themselves with a personal style and succeed in establishing themselves as distinct and self-sufficient individuals" (*La parola interdetta* 37).[18]

Tabucchi, a scholar of Portuguese literature, borrows from Fernando Pessoa this mode of radical self-examination in which body and voice are given to repressed personality traits, but overcomes the self-imposed solitude of the subject who observes and thinks about life rather than live it. As Tabucchi reminds us, Pessoa's elevation of the microcosm to macrocosm prevents the subject from looking outside itself. In his words, in Pessoa "the subject excludes the object, in fact, the subject becomes its own object, it is at once self and other. The other is no longer; it is supplanted by the alter ego: the heteronym" (*Un baule pieno di gente* 29).

Following Pessoa, Tabucchi explores the otherness within. However, Tabucchi utilizes the self-knowledge gained to better comprehend and interact with what is other—that is, everything that is external, and therefore potentially antagonistic, to the self. Recognition of the mutual determination and "necessary reciprocity" of self and other make for strengthened social bonds. In other words, radical introspection no longer prompts modernist atomization. Instead, the disarticulation of the *I* leads to a contestatory postmodern rediscovery of temporal and societal points of reference external to the self. Specifically, in *L'angelo nero* investigation of the meanders of the unconscious exceeds the parameters of the individual unconscious and the eternal present of postmodernity. In this work Tabucchi explores the conflict between individual conscious and unconscious as they interact with the collective dimensions of the perseverance of fascistic ideologies from the 1920s through their present-day consumerist incarnation.

For Tabucchi the logical consequence of the discovery of the other within is the reinvigoration of bonds of interdependence between an internally plural self and the external other. In his work the complementarity of self-knowledge and mutual understanding rests on an anticipation of the reciprocity of the gaze that Benjamin equates with "an experience of the aura to the fullest extent" (*Illuminations* 188). For Benjamin *aura* is intimately linked with an image of a past no longer retrievable in the present in its original form. What returns the gaze—for Benjamin it could be a person, an element of the natural world or an original (not mechanically reproduced) work of art—"conjures up" the past. "Experience [of aura], he avers, directly "corresponds to the data of the *mémoire involontaire*" (188). In other words, gazing at the other—Tabucchi would not distinguish between internal and external—frees what has been written out of history and unearths the latent remnants of the individual and collective unconscious.

In *L'angelo nero* the surrealistic self-analysis of the immanent narrator extends itself into an investigation of the historical inheritance of an entire people. Much like Benjamin's Angel of History, Tabucchi's angel, in his own words:

> Is an interior voice, one's conscience, memory. Memory too—he continues—can be an angel, because it brings back what no longer is, realities that no longer exist, that have been dissolved, but now return to encumber the present. [Borsari 5]

Tabucchi makes no secret of the relevance of surrealist narrative strategies to *L'angelo nero*. One need only look at the cover art (a reproduction of Brauner's *The Surrealist*) and the epigraph that couples the images of angel and puppet.[19] Moreover, equally important to Tabucchi's text as the surrealists' probe of the unconscious is the movement's explicit politics, specifically the fundamental relevance they attribute to lived praxis in their art. The surrealist sounding of the unconscious, according to Bonito Oliva, was born of the "exigency to bring artistic experience from the realm of the subjectivity of the *I* to the objectivity of the *We*." They hoped to accomplish this by allowing the *I* to function outside or through its own "egotic circle" until "it reached sociality and history" (107, 104–5). They understood—in the opinion of Roland Barthes—that "writing doesn't stop with the written, but can transmigrate into behavior, actions, activities, into private life, daily life, *what is done*" (*The Grain of the Voice* 245).

Building on this, we can say that any literary text, when it benefits from the aforementioned "complicity" of the reader, is capable of inserting itself in an esthetic-literary-social milieu to modify what reader response theory defines as the "horizon of expectation" of the reading public and, in some cases, the very structure of society.

The dialectical function of the text within such a "horizon of expectation" answers for Tabucchi broader queries regarding the social role of literature and its relationship to praxis, to then broach what for him is a more essential question: Why do writers write? In the essay "Equivoci senza importanza" (which plays on the title of an early collection of short stories, *Piccoli equivoci senza importanza*), Tabucchi contemplates the possibility that the primary motivation of writing is that of assuaging the guilt caused by what he considers a "false dilemma": the belief that in order to write, one must ineluctably choose between active participation in the social arena and hermetic, withdrawal from life into the realm of literature (109).[20]

As for what Tabucchi calls the question of the "fracture of art and life" raised but left unresolved by modernist literature,[21] in a scholarly article Tabucchi notes that the "inept antihero" represents one of "the principal arteries" of twentieth-century European literature. Specifically, he mentions the protagonists of "Joyce, Proust, Svevo, Musil, Pessoa, Pirandello, Kafka [and] Beckett," who all write about their inability to live":

> Writing and reflecting on the act of writing is the only "action" granted to this nullity; a mental life substitutes for real life, literature substitutes for reality. ["Àlvaro de Campos e Zeno Cosini" 151, 159]

Tabucchi then asserts that Pessoa, unlike many of the other writers just mentioned, discovered "a manner of finding reason and plausibility in a life that is very unreasonable and implausible" (151). However, Tabucchi's study of

Portuguese surrealist verse suggests to him the possibility of going beyond this relatively "positive vision" of the human condition and reestablishing "the link" between literature and life lost to the modernists, Pessoa included. Tabucchi explains that although a search for reality alternates in the work of the Portuguese surrealists with flight toward a belief in "the self-sufficiency of poetry" (*La parola interdetta* 22), because they never demonstrate the "stoic indifference" to the social and political conditions surrounding them, they do not propose a radical opposition between life and literature. Instead, one of the premises of the group's poetics, because of their total lack of expressive freedom under Salazarism, is the complete immersion in the imaginary as a means of achieving social incisiveness. In their lyrics the recovery of repressed psychic images constitutes a resistance to the rhetorical falsification of life.[22] At the same time, he is quick to note, neither one does find in the work of the Portughese surrealists a "*trait d'union* between poetry and life":

> You could say that they were denied an evident and explicit Marxist practice that operated subversively on bourgeois values; that it lacked a solid Freudian background to legitimate its theories: but fundamentally, it was the almost complete lack of liberty that forced it without appeal to be simple individual poetic expression. [9]

Nonetheless, the Portuguese surrealists do provide Tabucchi with a model of literary resistance to a "suffocating environmental situation" (8) that shares little with either the hero of classic realism or the modernist antihero. The surrealists' emotional and poetic involvement in their here and now becomes for him paragon of "everyman, as he struggles with life's most elementary problems and with hostile reality" (29). Following this example, Tabucchi recovers and investigates in *L'angelo nero* past traumata that are at once individual and collective in order to comment on a shared social and intellectual inheritance. Moreover, just as Pessoa devised "through himself, and only through himself, a novelistic universe" composed not in the "traditional" way with protagonist(s) and subordinate characters, but through a variety of heteronymic first-person narrators (Borsari 14), Tabucchi creates a composite narrator whose concerns regard both individual and—unlike Pessoa—the whole of society.

B. L'angelo nero

The stories of which *L'angelo nero* is composed are not autonomous narratives, but integrative parts that reciprocally enrich and condition the reading of the entire volume. Together they represent a cross section of the psychological baggage carried by Italians of Tabucchi's and successive generations. Through this objectifying multiplicity of perspectives, Tabucchi attempts, to use his phrasing, to somehow "placate the dead" ("Some Reflections on Translation" 7), that is, to exhume and respond to the unrecorded past. When a plurality of immanent narrators express and examine heteronymic manifestations of their own repressed traumata, the recuperated past transcends individual (auto)biography and speaks to the Italian intellectual's need to finally confront the literary, social, and political inheritance of the twentieth century.

The narratives make their way from Tabucchi's native Pisa ("Voci portate") through the Salazarist Portugal of his youth ("Notte, mare"), back to Italy—first the stagnant Italy of the postwar political restoration, then to a more contemporary one, characterized by the many *pentimenti* (acts of contrition) of terrorists who fashioned the "years of lead" of the late 1970s and early 1980s—to finally examine the psychological roots of the social, political, and cultural inheritance of Fascism ("Capodanno"). What Tabucchi has said of earlier collections of short stories he has written holds true for *L'angelo nero*: it is "in its own way a single tale" ("Equivoci senza importanza" 111).[23] This book, he says, "is a mosaic, a sort of novelistic universe. It is not a series of autonomous stories, because I do not like to write occasional stories" (Borsari 2).

In *L'angelo nero* the interrogation of the inheritance of the past articulates itself in the individual novelle through the reconstruction and analysis of the relationship of parental figures to characters more or less the same age as Tabucchi. The main characters of "Staccia buratta" and "La trota," for example, are negative portraits of writers who found an uneasy yet livable modus vivendi with the ideologies of Fascism and of its consumerist heir. Similarly, one of the central figures of "Il battere d'ali," a contemporary of the author, places economic well-being ahead of principle.

In contradistinction, Tadeus, the father figure of "Voci portate" and "Notte, mare," personifies a positive example of writers a generation Tabucchi's senior who resisted the dictatorial regimes that overtook much of western Europe in the 1920s and 1930s. Similarly, the immanent narrator of these two stories—a contemporary of Tabucchi—cannot rest until he has completed an exhaustive scrutiny of the forgotten past, a procedure ultimately completed in "Capodanno" where the protagonist (who, like Tabucchi, was born in Tuscany during the early 1940s) exhumes the collective traumata of Italians who came of age in the 1960s and 1970s.

In the first novella, "Voci portate da qualcosa, impossibile dire cosa," the return of the *I*'s repressed memories are initially catalyzed by the "voices" of the title and also by a pictorial representation of a "coot owl" (*folaga* [19]). Later on, in "Capodanno," the song of an owl will stimulate in the narrating persona a stream of memories; here, its plastic representation evokes for the reader "Voci giunte con le folaghe," a poem written by one of Italy's most prominant twentieth-century poets, Eugenio Montale—to whom Tabucchi makes explicit reference in his introductory "Note" (10).[24] While the allusions to Montale might lead one to sniff out a "postmodern" concern for metatextuality in this work (references to other authors are not lacking: passing acknowledgment is also made to Pessoa's "Chuva obliqua" [17], Pirandello's Mattia Pascal ["*Si fece credere morto per sfuggire*" (15)], and Calvino [the postulated equivalence of the *I*'s combinatoric word play and the tarots while at the Caffé Dante (18)][25]) metaliterature is by no means the main concern of this work. Instead, the "secret, childlike game" (13) of following the ebb and flood of *mémoires involontaires*, that is, of piecing together random thoughts (as they come together "to create something that did not exist and now exists: your story" [14]), of reappropriating through the act of writing a forgotten past in order to alter the course of the present are at the fore.

In "Voci portate da qualcosa, impossibile dire cosa," in addition to the metafictional "stories told by all those from whom you have stolen this one" (14), physical stimuli (for example, the cellar—metaphor of where his memories are stored—[21], the sundry gusts of wind [*folate*], the smell of brackish air [*aria salmastra* 16]) lead through the text to "Capodanno" where they will once again stimulate the recuperation of what lies hidden in the unconscious. Ultimately, in "Voci portate," the voice of a skinny male adolescent, who strongly resembles the protagonist of "Capodanno," will uncannily prompt the immanent narrator to hurry to the leaning Tower of Pisa (25) where he will by chance hear mention of *herpes zoster*, which can be metaphorically equated with the occasional resurfacing of feelings of remorse.[26] Other gusts of wind, and other physical stimuli, will trigger the return of other *mémoires involontaires* throughout this work.[27] All of them will join together in "Capodanno" to strike the *I* with the gale force of violent death when the little boy's perception of being "hit by a gust (*folata*) of frying onions" (129) is associated with sight of a small animal being butchered. Thus, contrary to what the title of the opening narrative would have us believe, it is not "impossible to tell" what uncannily restores forgotten memories of childhood traumata to consciousness.

The aggression of the persona and friends by the agent of the secret police in "Notte, mare" conjures up the oneiric image of the grouper which is associated in remembrance with both the black bottom of the lake from whence it "wriggles forth" and the black police cruiser. This particular image travels far beyond the setting of this brief narrative to "cross through walls and time; obstinate, unctuous, moribund but indefatigable: going forward, year after year, while life went on, years and years of it" (48–49), making its presence felt throughout the volume. In point of fact, fish imagery is central to "Capodanno" and links "Notte, mare" quite explicitly to the Montalean trout whose "wriggling" (*la trota che guizza*) "reminds me of your life." As Tabucchi explains, the image of the fish is borrowed from the surrealists and functions as a metaphor of the unconscious where "it lies at the bottom, in the mud, only occasionally appearing on the surface" (Borsari 20).

Like the allusions to Montale, the concern shown by the immanent narrator of "Staccia buratta" (a literary critic for a well-known periodical) for finding the right beginning for her autobiography raises in the reader questions regarding self-referentiality. However, it is very safe to say that the main thrust of the narrative lies elsewhere, specifically in Tabucchi's concern for the social repercussions of writing. In "Staccia buratta" the narrating persona, the only female *I* in the work, provides Tabucchi with a forum from which to comment on the state of the literary trade in Italy today, especially the determining presence of "reviewers and chroniclers given to a sort of call-criticism" (*critica-squillo* [Costanzo]), which fuels the creation and propagation of literary fashion. The *I* of "Staccia buratta" openly acknowledges her own lack of scruple and actively participates in what in Italy is currently referred to the neobaroque"[28] or postmodern vogue:

> Perhaps after a fashion, perhaps because in truth all writers had suddenly discovered within themselves a vein of

> avant-guarde inspiration, formal inventions, literary experimentation, or what was usually called "research" flourished. A period of adventures began. Because what really mattered was the adventure; when all was said and done, the books themselves did not count. What mattered was the searching, living that euphoric, fever-pitched moment, in which everything was exploding, the world, society, convention: even the words themselves exploded, even the words were frenzied and fever-pitched. [57–58]

It becomes ever clearer the extent to which her purely formalist concerns blend in memory with what she euphemistically calls her literary "conversion": the foresaking of a progressive avantgarde movement in order to embark on her professionally advantageous and lucrative "discovery" of Céline (58).

The remembrances of the second *laisse* of "Staccia buratta" are triggered by intimation, through the mnemic deformation of his name, to the volume's author. When the immanent narrator enters through "a door overshadowed by a tabacconist's sign" (*un'insegna di Tabacchi*)—made of an incongruous pink neon—she is assailed by "a strange fear" (59) that leads to the uncovering and inspection of childhood memories.[29] The question she asks herself at the outset, where to begin the recounting of her life, boils down to, first, whether she betrayed her youthful ideals and, second, pinpointing in time when this took place. Together, the word play on Tabacchi-Tabucchi and persona's metafictional equation of life and autobiography underscore the necessary imbrications in Tabucchi's work of self-analysis within the social context and interrogation of the act of writing with respect to the role of the writer in society.[30] The *I* of "Staccia buratta" is convinced she has abjured nothing. In point of fact, a decisive act of this nature might have granted her a more heroic dimension. Instead she cynically distorted the ideological and artistic rigor of her companion Beniamino[31] in order to gain admittance into the "pink light" district of facile, self-serving compromise in Italy's *mercato delle lettere* (Ferretti):

> Her column in the newsmagazine, for example, that was a real joke. With all that rubbish she had passed off as masterpieces, those senseless hodge-podges, rantings and ravings whose literary worth she had confirmed, that she had helped sell, that she had praised to the heavens. [61]

Thus, through the immanent narrator of this story, Tabucchi interrogates the function of the contemporary person of letters and the effects of a cowardice and lack of rigor that permit the past to be denied and responsibility for the ills of society to be eluded.

Although allusions to Tabucchi's *oeuvre* and autobiography are by no means lacking, they serve only to ground the narratives in a specific here and now so that they might be considered as symptomatic of the condition of the intellectual in contemporary Italy. Tabucchi is disinclined to define his work as overtly engaged; he professes not to address political events but rather the "psycological results it produces in his characters" (Mattei). His political commitment, he claims, is not "Sartrean," but of a moral, introspective, nature: a "complete and total honesty with oneself" ("Scrittori d'Italia" 85). Because his fictions raise the question of the *mal de vivre* and the "uneasiness" (*disagio*) he sees permeating society, they unavoidably acquire a collective dimension. Therefore, his narratives are of a contemporary, topical nature, "and the evil presences of which they speak are not fantastic, but real and psychological" (Borsari 2).

It should be clear that Tabucchi understands that in order to attend to "real, psychological problems," factors both internal and external to the individual must be considered. The act of writing allows him to execute what he calls a "double depersonalization" (Cigliana 33), which is, first, description in the third-person of another, and then the analytic depiction of the self from the perspective of (an)other. in his own words:

> [it is the] escape from the univocal and constrictive point of view called Antonio Tabucchi and the immersion in the point of view of a character that does not coincide with this *I* that is speaking but with an invented *I*. [La Porta 94]

The self heteronymically observes itself as other. At the same time, neither the perspective of the subject nor the more objective vantage of the other gain predominance, but instead a situation is created in which each defines and informs the other in a relationship of parity. Moreover, what at first glance strongly resembles "autobiographism," to use his terminology, is in fact "an operation of metabiography" (Belfiori). Writing about one's own life is not synonymous with life itself; rather, one writes about the process of analyzing the internal and external influences on individual lives.

The question raised by the title of "Il battere d'ali di una farfalla a New York può provocare un tifone a Pechino"—and cynically reiterated within the text by another secret police agent—is answered affirmatively in the dialogue by Carlo Emilio Gadda which it evokes.[32] Gadda, in "L'egoista" maintains that all life forms are united by inseparable bonds of interdependence. Tabucchi takes pains in "Il battere d'ali" to underscore the egoism inherent in narrations that willfully ignore fabulation's repercussions in the world. This short story depicts a conversation between a repentant terrorist and a political police agent. It drips with the confessional lexicon typical in Italy of the violent left- and right-wing extremists—and mafiosi—who betray their comrades-in-arms and tell special tribunals of their exploits outside the law.

Tabucchi's *pentito* masks behind artful fabrication what in truth is his self-serving, hypocritical complicity with a radically antidemocratic police action. The former terrorist takes pains to portray the dubious "passion and torment" (85) of his conscience (90), which, he claims, has caused him to "repent" (73) and "confess" (73): not to crimes he has in fact committed but to those mendaciously attributed to him by the political police.

The logical consequence of this unholy rebirth is his "baptism" as "Butterfly" (73). However, contrary to what the police agent avows, the ultimate goal of all this for "Butterfly" is not "expiation" (84), or assumption of guilt followed by reparation, but evasion. In this way, Tabucchi transforms the "quintessential Montalean image of the trapped butterfly" (Ahern 4), into a smalltime hoodlum who conveniently justifies and conceals his criminal activities behind an insincere patina of political idealism and revolutionary rhetoric.[33]

As is the case with the *I* of "Staccia buratta," for Butterfly "guilt" and "remorse" are associated with a *bar-tabacchi* (84). The site of the assassination to which he agrees to confess coincides with the *incipit* of his falsification of the past and—and this matters more—the impetus for the domino-effect of reciprocal, and fraudulent, accusations and incriminations the police wish to instigate. As the Man Dressed in Blue makes crystal clear, Butterfly's story is merely a piece in a puzzle designed by the police, a *petit récit* within their *grand* misrepresentation of the past. This issue, the relationship of writing to past praxis, will be addressed once again in "La trota che guizza."[34] The protagonist of "La trota" deliberately transmogrifies the past—denying and perverting his *ouevre*—an act Tabucchi describes as "wicked" (Décina Lombardi), due to his belief that writing is a means of "struggling against time" and of reappropriating the past (Borsari 11).

The concerns of the preceding stories, particularly the psycological inheritance of the past, the social role of the writer, and the interplay of individual and collective biography, come together in "Capodanno." In this concluding novella the present is continuously overtaken and interrupted by *mémoires involontaires*, which cut ever deeper into the past. Physical stimuli such as the singing of the cicadae uncannily spark the return of memories from the collective narrator's childhood while evoking the internal memory of the text, specifically the traumata already reconsidered in the other stories collected in the volume.

For example, the intratextual ties between "La trota che guizza" and "Capodanno" are quickly made apparent in the first paragraph of the latter story when, in an oneiric visit to the father's underwater tomb, the immanent narrator is overwhelmed by "wriggling fish" (*pesci guizzanti* [109]), an image reinforced later on by visions of wriggling lizards (135) and of the local fishermen's "*muscoli guizzanti*," as they labor in the brackish air of the shore (134). Moreover, the coupling of the image of the butterfly with sentiments of remorse first proposed in "Il battere d'ali" is re-inforced in "Capodanno" when the boy disobeys express orders from his mother and examines the contents of his late father's trunk—which contains memorabilia of the latter's service in Mussolini's army, evidence of the father's complicity in war crimes witnessed by the boy—and is overtaken by a swarm of butterflies (149).

The most critical problem the *I* must deal with is, in fact, defining his relationship to his father, a Fascist hierarch executed after the fall of Mussolini's puppet republic of Salò and given ignominious burial at the bottom of a lake by Resistance fighters. The boy's immaginary correspondent, Captain Nemo, according to Tabucchi, is symbolic of the relationship to the father (Borsari 19), an ambivalent mixture of "contempt and pity" (110). On a more conscious plane, the boy associates Nemo with both his favorite readings and first efforts at writing.

Because his description of Nemo ("incompetent and vile, a man who thinks only of his papers" [150]), is reminiscent of the protagonist of "La trota," we see how the focus of this story oscillates between a specific father-son dynamic and, metaphorically, analysis of the psychological and intellectual inheritance of Fascism on the one hand and, on the other, consideration of the relationship between writers more or less Tabucchi's age and their literary masters. In point of fact, for the hermetic poet of "La trota," writing is a "blinding flash of light" (*un abbaglio* [102]). In contrast, in "Capodanno" the act of writing is assigned a different synesthetic attribute, the sound of a torpedo gliding through water (150), which to the boy's mind equates writing and activism (not by chance this is the same sound the politically *engagé* Tadeus of "Notte, mare o distanza," associates with the composition of verse [34]).

L'angelo nero utilizes autobiographical and intertextual references to other works by Tabucchi in an attempt to resolve the "fracture between art and life" mentioned above while avoiding retreat toward the purely literary world of metafictional citationism that informs a certain stylistic definition of postmodernist narrative. Tabucchi does not consider the life of the artist metonym of a universal human condition, as is the case with late modernists such as Barth and Calvino. Rather, knowing how to write and knowing how to live intersect: both the author and his personae take stock of and profit from experiences common to both writing and living. The leitmotif of the destroyed manuscript in Tabucchi's work is indicative of this. It comes to epitomize the exigency that the untextualized past be reappropriated and the writer once again be an active, participatory agent in the world.' The immanent narrator of "*Storia di una storia che non c'è*" ["The Story of a Story That Is Not There"], collected in 1987 in *I volatili del Beato angelico* (58-61), tells of the annihilation of the typescript of a now "absent novel" (interestingly, in light of "Capodanno," entitled *Letters to Captain Nemo*, then *No One Behind the Door*). Moreover, Tabucchi has spoken in interviews of novels he has thrown page by page into the Atlantic rather than publish (see, for example, "Equivoci senza importanza" 110).

In the introductory "Note" to *L'angelo nero*, Tabucchi fictionalizes this autobiographical information while linking

"Capodanno" to the earlier, "absent" text by averring that this story is derived from "a novel [he] wrote many years ago and then threw away" (9). Further on, the persona of "Capodanno" makes oblique reference to another work by Tabucchi, *Piccoli equivoci senza importanza* (151) as he sets fire to the "insignificant phrases, things of no importance" that are his youthful attempts at creative writing, metaphor of an untextualized yet remembered past. At the same time, mention of the destroyed manuscript evokes a previous passage of the volume: the *I* of "Voci portate" is tormented by—among other things—the memory of having thrown a manuscript away (20).

Thus in "Capodanno" the internal memory of the text and references to Tabucchi's biography transform the past into something more, a living organism: "bacteria"—cultivated in the remains of a significantly "red" fish (151)—which is both symbolic of the past and meant to strike at the very heart of its negative ("black," Fascist) antecedents. Through this image, writing comes to absolve the function Tabucchi attributes to it: it is a means of acquiring knowledge of the self and understanding of the other (Belfiori). And we can add, it comes to constitute a dialectical antithesis within the reader's horizon of expectation to the "continuous present" of postmodernity.

Afterword

Living the Flux of Postmodernity

The rapid progress made in telecommunications and information technology during the last quarter century is at the root of the shortened time horizons of postmodernity. The difficulty of elaborating a response that is not easily commodified and assimilated into a single world economic system is compounded by the pervasive influence of the mass media who paradoxically contribute to both the unraveling of the social fabric and the inculcation of conformistic behavior. Thus, the question of living the flux of uncertainty characteristic of postmodernity becomes one of, to borrow Toni Morrison's phrasing, making "criteria and knowledge . . . emerge outside of the categories of domination" (*Playing in the Dark* 7). This is particularly problematic because no external Archimedean point exists for such an endeavor and contestation is caught between the need to think locally, responding to the needs of heterogeneous groups and identities, while acting globally.

I have concentrated on individual authors and their narrative strategies, rather than the expressly political aspects of the postmodern debate and the process of formation of a hegemonic "collective will" (Gramsci) because we come to know the world through our narration of it. Literature is capable of contesting "postmodern culture," because it is more than mere illustration or document. Literature intervenes in history with its own authentic force, transforming vital and historical forces and experiences into artistic tension first and then into works of art (Binni) which are capable of modifying the "horizon of expectation" of its public. When the contestatory narratives discussed in chapter six recuperate and undermine univocal readings of the past, they suggest ways of reversing the postmodern flattening of temporality within the ephemeral dimensions of the broadcasted image.

When oppositional narratives and their readers attempt to guide the course of postmodernity, they acknowledge what metafiction would conceal: the absent author. When the experience of another is recovered through the act of reading, certain contents of the reader's past "combine with material of the collective past" (Benjamin, *Illuminations* 159), shattering the isolation of the reader. Therefore, what has been proposed above as a means of redirecting the development of postmodernity toward more livable, human dimensions is a heterotelic narrative transitivity—an active reimmersion of narrative in the social—which contrasts sharply with the autotelic concern for their own procedures and the hermetic intransitivity of modernist self-consciousness and late modernist self-reflexivity. The reader gains through interaction with contestational narratives a critical vantage outside the continuous present installed in postmodernity: the acquisition of objectifying points of reference external to the self makes possible the reappropriation of the past and, as a consequence, the reorientation in time of the subject.

Perhaps the most apparent symptom of the manner and extent to which the continuous present is installed in postmodernity, is the journalistic effacement of the temporal depth of lived experience. In his essay on Baudelaire, Benjamin decries the manner in which the "lack of connection between news items" in the daily papers prevents the reader from assimilating the information they supply. Events of major import are separated from their historical context—their causes and consequences—and offered as commodities to be quickly consumed and forgotten. The news seems to exist independently of the personal-historical situations of both reporter and public. It cannot be a means for knowing the world, because the recounted events remain alien to the individual. Even the limiting case of crime news (rapes and murders in one's own neighborhood, for example) is presented as little more than a collection of sundry "happenings" and curiosities, cause for hysteria, perhaps, but not for reflection on the roots of society's ills and the direction of its development. When events are presented as a chronicle, their endurance in consciousness is only commensurate to their "shock value."[1]

As a consequence, the information imparted, unlike shared "experience," cannot and does not transform its audience. In postmodernity, the emptying of content from the news is accentuated by the new technologies that are much less encumbered by their means of distribution than the print media. Television news makes social, economic, and cultural realities much more visible, or "transparent" (to use Vattimo's term[2]), than ever before, but does little to make them more intelligible: insight into the historical development of social forces is occluded by their presentation as trends.[3]

The leveling of time by the media in postmodernity finds its literary counterpart in the "citation" of canonical works by ludic metafictionists whose "ironic" rewriting of the past effectively condenses and absorbs it into the present. The use of erudite citations in metafiction detaches works of different periods from their here and now, and integrates them into the present of the reader. Literature thus would abstain from investigating anything other than static, circumscribed totality of knowledge whose readers learn only that which they already know (the books they have previously read and now recognize in the metafictional text). The collapse of time in metafiction occludes the historical referent to which the canonical work was a direct response. By the same token, it consoles and habituates the reader to the present, and contributes to the atrophy of the will and ability of the reader to interrogate world and self. It does so by illuding readers that his/her specific identity is protected from anonymity within massified society by creating a sense of belonging to a separate community of intellectual elites, each of whom enjoys literate citations and is capable of creating his/her own individualized text. Within the self-contained, literary world of metafiction order is restored and closure attained.[4] The world is not questioned by metafiction, but enjoyed just as it is. In this way, "Model Readers" and their metafictionist authors collude to conceal what reader and world could be but are not and forestall interrogation of and new insight into the structures of reality.

John Barth's loosely autobiographical Genie explicitly ascribes to his metafictional writings a consolatory function.[5] To that same end (that of dehistorizing and rendering docile the text) Umberto Eco—despite his announced intent of "transforming" the reader—utilizes a much more subtle and articulated argumentation. According to Eco, the "open text" offers itself to multiple readings. However, while it abstains from "validating" any one interpretation, it conditions and limits all possible readings. In a second phase, according to Eco, the "open text" is "created" by the self-validating interpretations of his "model reader."

It should be clear that, as is the case with Calvino's "dead author," Eco's "open text" is a ruse. The reader is mislead into believing that the author has ceded authority over the text, but this is not the case. The metafictionist feigns death in order, as Eco phrases it, to "repressively direct reader cooperation" (*Lector in fabula* 60). Authors do not die, but, quite to the contrary, hide inside their texts.[6] The emphasis placed by the metafictionist on the interaction of text and reader interpretation forestalls consideration of authorial intent (who, Eco jokes, "should die after having written. So as not to disturb the progress (*cammino*) of the text ["Postille" 509]), thereby redefining for Eco "the still valid hermeneutic circle" ("Intentio lectoris" 39–40). As Eco affirms, a hermeneutic reading disregards the here and now of the work and, by divorcing the work from its historical context, makes the work itself the only criterion for analysis. He prefers this strategy of reading/interpreting because, in his own words, consideration of authorial intent and of "so-called writings of poetics do not always help understand the work that inspired them." In his opinion, they serve only, and not always, to help understand after the fact how the technical problems associated with the production of a work of art were resolved ("Postille" 509).

Moreover, Eco considers the "open text" "socially incisive" because it "transforms" the reader, who is modified through the act of reading-interpreting (*Lector in fabula* 45). Since the "Model Reader" is "not to think of anything at all except what the text offer[s]" ("Postille" 523), it is safe to assume that this "transformation" is catalyzed by the reader's self-authenticating interpretations of the text. These are the result of the interplay between an understanding of the work's component parts and an evolving sense of the whole.

Binni, however, has refuted such reasoning, magisterially affirming the importance of comprehending the poetic intentions of the author. There, the work and the literary and nonliterary questions that permeate the production of the text, and their transmutation in artistic tension and direction within a specific and unrepeatable historical contingency, are brought together (20). In other words, analysis of the poetics of the author evokes an absence—and through that absence, the experience of another. Then, through the "complicity of text and reader" (Costanzo), the past can be dialogically integrated into the experience of the reader, modifying the reader's "horizon of expectation" in the present and behavior in the future. Cognizance of each text's historical specificity prevents literary "exhaustion"—because it recognizes that an integral part of the internal dynamic of every work is its here and now. Therefore, the past can be revisited, and without irony, because it may resemble the present, but is never replicated by it.

In ludic or esthetic responses to postmodernity, the implied intent behind the "rethinking" (Eco) and "replenishing" of an "exhausted" (Barth) past, according to Eco, is to "not only identify the causes in the past of what happened later," but also to "make history, what happened, more clearly understood" ("Postille" 532). Thus, it becomes clear that for Eco "what really happened" in the past can be ascertained and made a synchronic part of the present, because it is synonymous with what is preserved in texts.

I contend that the text signifies a liberating absence—that of the author—that makes available to the reader the alternative memory of another. The text is there where its author is not. As Blanchot writes, the author's absence is an active one (158) and the text a space "where what is no longer still subsists" (145). Thus, the literary text is not only a storehouse of individual memory, but also a source of collective remembrance capable of evoking traces of subaltern pasts that have been written out of causal or linear narratives of history. The acknowledgment of this latent presence can charge events, giving them a direction unforeseen by narratives that "write history backward" (Kuhn), reducing the past to a function of the present.

Unlike the "postmodern attitude" cited by Eco—which is characterized by the supplanting of life by literature (through the subordination of the real events referred by the narrative to the act of narration) and the literary encumbering of the present to the point that one's most profound utterances, such as a declaration of love, come not from the heart but "disingenuously" from a cited text ("Postille" 529)—the concept of the text as absence allows us to draw on the reservoir of collective memory of which literature is a part, confront our experiences with those of others, and embed them imaginatively in our own. This does not prevent our experiencing life ingenuously, as Eco maintains. To the contrary we can live with greater intensity because of the heightened self-awareness and greater appreciation for those experiences reading affords.

When literature gives access to collective memory, it suggests a way out of the solitude inflicted on the subject of postmodernity by the "totalizing and totalitarian Moloch" (Paternostro, "I perché degli incontri"[13]) that laissez faire postmodernity is capable of becoming. The new technologies radically alter the individual's relationship to the now spatially and temporally boundless work place: cellular phones and fax machines put the worker on call twenty-four hours a day. Moreover, computer and television monitors make an immense quantity and variety of information available while packaging it to fit the individuality of the consumer.

The long-term effects of the combination of informational saturation and narrow-casting are, paradoxically, an increased pressure on the individual to conform to the media's definition of mainstream opinion on the one hand and, on the other, greater a weakening of community bonds (Wolf, *Gli effetti sociali* 188). Furthermore, an alternative perspective, which facilitates critical thinking, becomes accessible when a historical perspective is acquired through recognition of authorial absence. The "necessary reciprocity" of the literary and the socio-economic spheres makes viable the use of narrative responses as models of opposition while delegitimating the metafictionist's retreat from the world. By establishing an albeit tenuous line of demarcation between modern and postmodern narratives—through a purposely nonprescriptive description of diverse, partial solutions—we may learn how to better live the flux of uncertainty endemic to postmodernity.

As we have seen, narrative strategies for recuperating multiple forms of otherness diverge. While Doctorow undermines objectivity, Morrison utilizes an objectifying plurivocity, and Tabucchi multiple subjectivities. Underlying these responses—in contradistinction to the disoriented, radical subject-centricity of high and late modernist strategies—oppositional postmodernist narrations of narrations find a measure of unity in their syntheses of heterogeneities, thereby suggesting forms of dialogic resistance to both the homologating tensions of massified society and the dispersive political particularisms that occlude the common interests shared by diverse oppressed groups. Thus, their source of strength is not to be found in a radical historical relativism (for example, Vattimo's "heterotopia" of multiple "weak ontologies," which plays into the hands of the unabashedly "strong ontology" of global capitalism) but in the awareness of historical relativity to be gained through dialogic comprehension of the other.

My juxtaposition of modernist and postmodernist responses to the world in the preceding chapters hopefully suggests possibilities for narratives that do not passively reflect nor ludically succumb to their context, as is the case with late modernist metafictions. Rather, the desire to know, contest, and transform the postmodern world will hopefully contribute to the opening up of ever larger spaces for informed democracy and emancipation.

Notes

Chapter 1

1. What Benjamin proposes is quite different from Vattimo's "archaeological" mining of the past. The postmodernist "overcoming" of historical progression, according to Vattimo, allows being to be conceived as a succession of "archeological" recuperations of disconnected "events." They are not "emplotted," to borrow Hayden White's term, but merely "remembered" and "hermeneutically described" without reference to the here and now of either the narrator or the narrated (Vattimo, "*Postmodernità*," 101). This compression of the past within the present is reminiscent of the metafictional conflation of past and present. I will discuss this in greater detail in the Afterword.

2. To explain, literary modernism moved away from the objective, public space of nineteenth-century realism and toward the privatization of experience. The late modernist carries this tendency to its extreme. In the work of high modernists such as Pirandello and Svevo, the subject of narrative does not live life as much as think about it and then write about his thoughts. Late modernists are concerned less with life and more with the act of writing, and so they write about writing.

3. The Italian critic Remo Ceserani considers, as do I, Calvino a modernist and Tabucchi a postmodern writer, but for different reasons. In Ceserani's opinion, Tabucchi's work is an

example of what Lentricchia calls "progressive postmodernism" based on the presence "of typical [stylistic] features of postmodern literature" (380). These features include "the themes of the double or ambiguous personality, the consubstantiality of love and hatred, the experience of despair and solitude . . . the importance of dreams, childhood fixations, and all the obsessions of literature, the open-ended plot that at times reverses itself and gets caught in a sort of Gödel's knot . . . the problematization of points of view and narrative perspectives, the nostalgic evocation of certain periods in recent history . . . the weakening or multiplication of the subject." Calvino, on the other hand, according to Cesarani "belongs firmly to the tradition of modernity, because "his frame of mind remained to the very end that of an enlightened intellectual whose experiments with narrative techniques and points of view were substantially those of high Modernism; Calvino's conception of language was that of a transparent vehicle of communication" (39). Ceserani's use of stylistic criteria leads Ceserani to list along with other examples of postmodern writers Umberto Eco. In the Afterword that follows this text I will associate the "citationism" of *Il nome della rosa* with the late modernist metafiction of Calvino and Barth.

Chapter 2

1. Ferretti does well to underscore the manner in which Calvino creates for his readership a self-image of his intellectual and literary development as something complete and self-contained. Ferretti casts in relief the writer's unwillingness to speak of works in progress—as if he were reticent "*not show his hand*" so that he might "recompose after the fact and present to the public a unitary and resolved image" (55–56).

2. Calvino told Scalfari ("*Quel giorno i carri*") that the roots of his disenchantment with politics extended back to 1956: "Those events estranged me from political, in the sense that previously politics had occupied a much greater part of me. After that I no longer considered it a totalizing activity; I lost faith in it."

3. This and all translations from the Italian are mine.

4. As Dombroski has synthesized, "in communicating images, poets solve certain technical and structural problems that are extrinsic to art proper. Croce distinguishes between a "technique" relative to the reproduction or communication of the image. As a result, history (politics and culture) and material practices (the painting, writing, or compositional processes) remain subordinated to artistic creation as elements of practical rather than theoretical necessity" (*Antonio Gramsci* 15–16).

5. In "*Fauna de los Estados Unitos*: Borges writes, "the ludic mythology of the foresters of Wisconsin and Minnesota includes singular creatures in whom, surely, no one has ever believed." Specifically, "the *Hidebehind* is always to be found behind something. No matter how many times a man turns around, the Hidebehind is always in back of him and that is why no one has ever seen him, even though he has killed and devoured many woodcutters" (*Manual de zoología fantástica* 74).

6. The thematic core of the other stories in *Le cosmicomiche* is furnished by the binary opposition of identities, "self/other" or "us/them." For example, in "*I Dinosauri*" the world is divided into a dominant group and its ethnic other (121). "*Lo zio acquatico*" is a throwback to a previous, more traditional civilization in conflict with the modern land-bound civilization of those who emigrated from the sea to the firmament. In "*Senza colori*" identity is defined by place of residence: the organic and mineral (65) exist either *al di qua* or *al di là* (hither or yon) of the earth's surface (73–74).

7. One need only think of the text that paradigmatically reflects the worldview that emanates from Pirandello's *oeuvre, Uno, nessuno e centomila*. Vitangelo Moscarda, Pirandello's protagonist, was concerned with the identities created for him independently of his will by those who observed and interacted with him.

8. In *Cosmicomiche vecchie e nuove* the subheading "*La memoria del mondo*" will be transformed into "*La memoria dei mondi*." The plurality serves to underline the further distancing from previous anthropomorphic contexts.

9. The OULIPO (*l'Ouvroire de Littérature Potentielle*) was a group formed by the French writer Raymond Queneau of ten people who carried out mathematic-literary experiments and re-

search (see "Chi cattura chi?"). For a more detailed discussion of combinatory literature, see Motte.

10. Combinatorics allowed Calvino to look beyond what was for him a superficial chaos, mere appearance, to seek out a unifying coordination of phenomena. As he told Camon in 1973, he was seeking a "grand system . . . in which any alteration sparks a series of alterations until a new equilibrium is reached" (199). Given a cast of characters and a basic story premise, a computer could be called on to generate an infinite number of stories "and then select those few realizations compatible with certain constraints" ("Prose and Anticombinatorics" 143). The writer-programmer would then seek out a symmetry, the most plausible minitotality within the computer-generated grand narrative. In 1967 Calvino stated his preference not for "the explanation of an extraordinary fact, but rather the *order* that this extraordinary fact develops within and around itself," the design, the symmetry, the network of images that are deposited around it in a manner resembling the formation of a crystal" (Ups 216).

11. This is the title given to this suite of stories in *Cosmicomiche vecchie e nuove*.

12. It should be added parenthetically, the traditional, stereotypical gender roles and allegorical behavior that animates this particular story permeates the cosmicomic narratives. In "*I cristalli*," for example, men are the producers, their wives the idle consumers.

13. This, of course, is directly related to the theme of "*La memoria del mondo*"—that is, the historiographic use, misuse, and abuse of texts and artifacts. In "*La memoria del mondo*," which appears only in this collection and represents a path quickly abandoned, the narrating *I* is charged with the selection, organization, and storage of the world's memory. Therefore, only he may determine what is to be historicized and preserved, and what will be effaced. Like the Abbot Faria, the narrative voice of "*La memoria del mondo*" includes only "what is, what was, and what will be" at the expense of all unrealized potentialities (170) in what posterity will believe is an objective historiography, a grand narrative of History (with a capital H). Instead, behind the illusion,

he imposes his own "personal imprint on the world's memory" (170), condensing and even falsifying on whim.

Chapter 3

1. For Barth, Calvino's *Le cosmicomiche* and *Il castello dei destini incrociati* were "exemplary postmodernist" works (*The Friday Book* 196) because in these two texts Calvino kept "one foot in the narrative past" while bringing forth a "transcendent parody" of the literary tradition (204). In contradistinction, *Le città invisibili*, presumably because of its fragmentary, introspective nature, was considered by Barth a typically "modernist" text. For Calvino's interest in Barth's work, see Lucente, 252.

2. This disengaged view of metafiction is not contradicted by Barth, for whom an aversion to committed art coincides with an explicit search for "esthetic bliss." Federman lists both Barth and Calvino among those writers who to his mind are "more concerned with the problems of writing their books, of letting the difficulties of writing fiction transpire in the fiction itself, rather than commit themselves the problems of Man and the injustices of society" (*Critifiction* 5). Calvino, it must be noted, remained to the end a much more *engagé* writer than the one depicted by Federman, although such a description does tend to corroborate the "waning of Calvino's future-oriented social project" discussed elsewhere in this volume.

3. Since life is written, the basic units of Barth's frametales are those of writing, the "couple dozen squiggles we can write with our pen" (*Chimera* 8), not those of the oral tradition.

4. The modernist desire to mediate fundamental conflicts of values between diverse worlds is egregiously present, for example, in the reconciliation of the radically diverse value systems of Genie and Scherazade in Barth's "Dunyadiade" (*Chimera* 16). The modern-day Genie can frame Dunyazade's tale in one quick stroke by fictionalizing further and corroborating her narrative, while "replenishing" the literary tradition through the recycling of its basic materials.

Chapter 4

1. The structure of the work can be depicted in the following manner:

```
^
^
C                                                     na ** na na na nascoste*
I                                               co ** co ** co co continue
V                                         c  ** c  ** c  ** c  cielo
I                                   mo ** mo ** mo ** mo ** morti
L                             n  ** n  ** n  ** n  ** nome
I                       o  ** o  ** o  ** o  ** occhi
Z                 sc ** sc ** sc ** sc ** scambi
A           so ** so ** so ** so ** sottili
T        s  s  ** s  ** s  ** segni
I     d  d  d  ** d  ** desiderio
O* m  m  m  m  ** memoria
N     I           II    III   IV     V    VI    VII   VIII  IX

   Time >>                                             * = Polo-Kan dialogs
```

2. In this regard, see Cannon, "Italo Calvino: The Last Two Decades" 64 and *Crisis of Reason* 102.

3. In *Il castello*, Motte writes, "Calvino returns to his highly personalized vision of the origins of narrative. In this sense, the narrative activity in *The Castle of Crossed Destinies* takes place in an edenic state, where words have not yet come along to corrupt stories. For Calvino suggests that words are by their very nature lapsarian constructs, fallen and imperfect tools. The image, on the other hand, is pure and (more important) *original*; it is, therefore, an adequate vessel for the story it contains. Contiguous to this argument is the notion of the materiality of the image, which Calvino opposes to the ephemeral character of the word" (125).

4. Although Calvino does not make specific reference to the Russian Formalists in this essay, what he proposes is highly reminiscent of Shklovsky's concept of "defamiliarization," for whom "the purpose of art is to force us to notice. It does so by impeding perception or, at least calling attention to itself" (Lemon and Reis 4).

5. In this context, the act of reading is considered "a process of abstraction or rather an extraction of concreteness from abstract operations ("The Written and the Unwritten Word" 39). What Calvino says here about reading is consistent with his equation in 1964 of the act of reading and the visive appropriation of reality: "each book we read when young is like a new eye that opens and modifies the sight of the other eyes or book-eyes that we already had" (*Il sentiero dei nidi di ragno* 17). The application of this "phenomenological approach to the world" is perhaps best described in Calvino's recounting of his experience in a Tokyo train station. After an initial feeling of disorientation, he wrote, "I will begin to no longer find noteworthy, to *no longer see* what is in front of my eyes. To see means to perceive differences, and as soon as differences become foreseeable and uniform, something we are accustomed to seeing, the gaze begins to slide along a smooth surface. Travel . . . helps us re-activate for a brief moment the use of our eyes, permitting a visual reading of the world" (Cds 168).

6. In the third of the "*Definizioni di territori*" ("*Il fantastico*"), Calvino explains how the narrator selects from within the preexisting totality of potential crystalizations, the most appropriate to then generate a new totality: "at the center of narration, in my opinion, is not the explanation of an extraordinary fact, but the *order* that this extraordinary fact develops within and around itself, the design, the symmetry, the network of images that are deposited around it, in a manner resembling the formation of a crystal" (Ups 216).

7. For Franco Ricci, despite the cards' marginal location, it is the verbal narration that "accompanies the figures on the cards in the margin" (193). In his words, "the narrative world of *The Castle of Crossed Destinies* pretends to averbality: it is an ideogrammatic world, a world dominated by the nonverbal sign. Or rather, it is a preverbal world, as Calvino insists upon both the temporal and the logical priority of the image" (125).

8. Ricci has indicated in his discussion of *Il castello dei destini incrociati*, "reality, once visualized by Calvino, is transformed by the author's imagination into a suitable, though supplemental, verbal expression" (202). Leube has also argued that Calvino demonstrates a "paradoxically, for an author, hier-

archical" relationship between the figurative and the literary (1203).

9. In a 1979 interview Calvino reiterated his dislike of the word's "generic" and "approximate" nature (D'Eramo 138). See also Camon (183) where Calvino expresses his "disgust" for the "ephemeral" spoken word.

10. Smart defines *chosisme* as an often repeated focus on objects characteristic of the *nouveau roman*. "At the same time," he writes, "human involvement in the perception of this 'objective' world is decreased, often to the point of creating an apparent narrative anonymity" (5).

Chapter 5

1. In *Collezione di sabbia* Calvino speaks directly to this concept. Following Barthes, he asserted that a *mathesis singularis* would be "a science for the uniqueness of every object . . . whose purpose is the definition of the singular and unrepeatable" (83).

2. Calvino told Nascimbeni that he planned to dedicate a chapter of this work to sight because humanity had become "used to reading and interpreting fabricated images, and has lost the primitive's ability to distinguish details, traces, and clues."

3. In the Tornabuoni interview Calvino said that "Il modello dei modelli" was a chapter on politics: "There was a time when Palomar thought he could construct a perfect, logical, geometrical model of society. After having perused all possibilities (should reality fit the model, or should the model fit reality?), he tries to see reality directly, without models."

Chapter 6

1. As Lester has written, Morrison's politics of alliance is constituted by a refusal to choose "between the black movement and women's liberation" and to see the two within a general sys-

tem of class oppression of all races and both genders, whose only beneficiary is the ruling class (52–53).

2. Bono and Kemp define symbolic placement as the "practice of reference and address, even a lineage or tradition within which to situate oneself in past, present and future" (12).

3. This comes in explicit opposition to what she perceives as modernism's conflicting tendencies to disfamiliarize and estrange black dialect through "deliberately unintelligible spellings" on the one hand and, on the other, to integrate and domesticate a "hip" urbane" idiom into standard American English (*Playing in the Dark* 52).

4. Consisting in this case of an epistemology, as she puts it, "discredited not because it is not true or useful . . . but because it is information held by a discredited people" ("Memory, Creation, and Writing" 388).

5. The most striking example of the lack of omniscience is realized in the sequence of events leading up to Sethe's assault on her benefactor, Bodwin: "Sethe feels her eyes burn and it *may have been* to keep them clear that she looks up" (261, my emphasis). At the same time, Beloved's internal life is always refractory to our gaze. Her inscutability is signaled soon after her appearance at Sethe's home: "she lifted her eyes to meet Denver's and frowned, perhaps. Perhaps not. The tiny scratches on her forehead may have made it seem so" (75).

6. In Morrison's own words, Beloved "is a spirit on one hand, literally she is what Sethe thinks she is, her child returned to her from the dead. And she must function like that in the text. She is also another kind of dead which is not spiritual but flesh, which is, a survivor from a true, factual slave ship. She speaks the language, a traumatized language, of her own experience" (Darling 6).

7. Nan "used different words. Words Sethe understood then but could neither recall nor repeat now. She believed that must be why she remembered so little before Sweet Home except singing and dancing and how crowded it was. What Nan told her she had forgotten, along with the language she told it in. The same language her ma'am spoke, and which would never come back" (63)

8. Moreover, Beloved's contacts with speakers of English were not frequent enough for her to acquire mastery. Hence, her speech both reflects an incomplete "internalization of the master's tongue" ("Friday on the Potomac" xxv) and retains some of the musicality and the cadence of her native language (*Beloved* 60).

9. As Rubenstein has indicated, names are "emblems of the black community's resistance to the white culture's negation of its world" (154).

10. Beloved's dreams are of her body exploding or being dismembered, and of being swallowed (133). Sethe, for that matter, has "undreamable dreams" (251) of fragmentation (272).

11. When Beloved hides from Denver, the latter bemoans her lack of self (123).

12. Because of the absence of her father, or any other male figure in her life, Denver's dream about a running pair of shoes (257)—which causes her to wake up frightened—may be indicative of a stunted sexuality (in Freud's dream analysis, shoes and slippers symbolize the female genital organs [Freud 140]).

13. To clarify this by example, in *The Waterworks* the medical histories of the children used in Sartorius's experiments demonstrate that Sartorius did their health no harm and yet it is known that they were literally scared to death by the fate that awaited them (233). The texts, although factual, do not reflect what is known to be true.

14. The effects of the homologation and stifling of multiple truths is evidenced in *The Waterworks* by Sartorius's exposition of the transmogrification of the democratic ideals on which the republic was founded. The democratic "mythic being" of the American people is violated when onto a founding myth such as that of the rugged individual is grafted a form of social Darwinism, which results in a perversion of the ideals of liberty, justice, and equality. Survival of the fittest comes to signify survival of the wealthiest, and liberty becomes that of the economically strong to deny justice and equality to individuals less fit for survival than they.

15. To clarify this point, in *The Waterworks* the facade of a univocal metanarrative of history is sabotaged by the very imma-

nent narrator whose story has for years lain hidden "invisibly in the same lines" of the newspaper he edited (65).

16. His dismissal from the newspaper "disempower[ed]" him (177) and put his life in a state of "suspension" (175).

17. I thank Tom O'Neill of the University of Melbourne for providing me with a typescript of this paper.

18. I have examined elsewhere the importance of Pessoa for Tabucchi, please see my "The Postmodern Discourses of Doctorow's *Billy Bathgate* and Tabucchi's *Dialoghi mancati*" and especially "L'eteronimia di Antonio Tabucchi." For the recuperation-rejection of Montale's "stoic resignation," a topic that will gain in significance further on in this chapter, I refer the reader to my "Tabucchi: una conversazione plurivoca."

19. The epigraph is taken from Rilke's *Duino Elegies*: "Engel und Puppe: dann ist endlich Schauspiel" (*Angel and doll: then it is finally the play*). While the angel evokes Benjamin, puppets, because they embody both human and nonhuman qualities, constituted for the surrealists "avatars of the uncanny confusion of life and death" (Foster *Compulsive Beauty* 121), a concept fundamental to *L'angelo nero*.

20. The perception of this "dilemma" indicates the extent to which the postwar discussions of Gramsci's *Prison Notebooks* and the question of engaged literature are to this day very much an implied presence in Italian literary discussions. It is also symptomatic of Tabucchi's own post-Neorealist formation—evinced in his attempts in his first novels, *Il piccolo naviglio* and *Piazza d'Italia* to reconstruct the "social identity" of Italians of his generation.

21. To gain some perspective, it is best to keep in mind what was said of Calvino's late modernism and the way in which the opposition of writing and political engagement was dealt with in his *Castle of Cross Destinies*. Calvino's immanent narrator, unlike the high modernists we are discussing in this paper, is not "inept." He does not write because he is incapable of living. Neither is writing a surrogate for life: rather, in Calvino—I have said the same of John Barth—the act of writing and living are synonymous. Calvino's reduction of the writer to archetype of himself elevates the condition of the writer to metaphor for a

universally human condition. As was the case with Pessoa, the microcosm becomes the macrocosm. As will be made clearer as my discussion of Tabucchi continues, in this isolation of the individual from the social context lies the primary distinction between modernist writing, high and late, and its oppositional postmodern counterpart.

22. Interestingly—I want to introduce this here because of its significance for *L'angelo nero*—symbol of the victory of poetry over the "false life" under the dictatorship is the fish. In this regard Tabucchi specifically cites the poem "Sigamos o cherne" (*Let's Follow the Grouper*) by Alexandre O'Neill (*La parola interdetta* 25. This poem is reprinted and translated into the Italian by Tabucchi in this same volume on pp. 188–89).

23. Tabucchi, in fact, had this to say about the plot, or lack thereof, of *L'angelo nero*: "When I write a book, I naturally produce a plot. But I do not think we are talking about a classic, nineteenth-century plot. My plot comes forward in bits and pieces" ("Scrittori d'Italia" 83).

24. It must be stressed that the references to Montale (including the protagonist of another of the stories collected in *L'angelo nero* [*"La trota che guizza"*] who very much resembles the Nobel laureate), symbolic of a generation's separation of politics and culture in order to live under Fascism innocuously (or, in Tabucchi's words, with "noble stoicism and resignation" [*I volatili del Beato angelico* 10]), as is the case with other physical stimuli and eidetic images utilized in *L'angelo nero*, binds the individual narratives through the internal memory of the text.

25. In the Borsari interview (10–11) Tabucchi speaks of Calvino's personal and professional influence on his writing. Interestingly, Tabucchi quotes Calvino's *Se una notte d'inverno un viaggiatore* in the search for an *incipit* that propels "Staccia Buratta." I refer the reader to the *laisse* of this novel by Calvino that begins on p. 153: ("To begin. You are the one who said it, dear reader. But how to establish the exact moment in which a story begins?")

26. To decipher this image, I must avail myself of another work by Tabucchi. In *Requiem* the immanent narrator views *Le*

Tentazioni di Sant'Antonio by Bosch "in which are depicted a fat man and an old woman who travel through the sky riding on a fish" (74), commonly—but mistakenly, according to another observer—held to be a grouper. The narrator learns from his companion that originally the painting had a thaumaturgic value. It was hung in the hospital of the Antonian Brothers in Lisbon, an institute for people afflicted with skin diseases, usually caused by some form of venereal disease, "the terrible Saint Anthony's Fire, which is what they used to call that contagious skin disease." The *I*'s interlocutor then goes on to explain that St. Anthony's Fire is an excruciating illness that "returns periodically and the infected area is filled with disgusting and very painful soars, . . . it is a virus called herpes zoster." His companion then tells him, "I think that herpes is a little bit like remorse, it lies sleeping inside us and then one day it wakes up and attacks us, then it goes back to sleep because we are able to calm it down, but it is always inside us, nothing can be done about remorse" (79).

27. For example, the Montale look-alike protagonist-poet of "La trota che guizza" advances toward death on "time that swayed like gusts of wind" (102). In "*Notte, mare o distanza*" memory of an agent of the Portuguese political police arrives on "an evil wind" (35), which rouses in the immanent narrator more and less conscious recollections of past examples of his own child-like helplessness in the face of acts of aggression. His memory is "paralyzed" by "a stronger gust of that awful, freezing wind" (42), which is associated with his absence from or cowardly presence at (memory is uncertain) the scene of conflict. Another gust of wind carries him back to his safeguard, a park twenty blocks away (44). Another significant intratextual link can be individuated in the disparaging use of diminutives by the agent of the *Polícia Internacional Defesa Estado*: in one particular instance, they feel "in that incongruous diminutive there was a compact violence, they felt it, something foul and evil that hit them in the shoulders like a gust of freezing wind and made them tremble" (38). This sentiment is not unlike what is felt by the *I* of "Capodanno" as he remembers "when they used to call him Cino" (118), a term of endearment for Duccio, and when he was afraid of dreaming of his father's body "at the bottom of a lake" bitten by fish with pointed teeth (119).

28. According to Caesar, in Italian literary criticism "the idea of the postmodern has scarcely taken hold at all" except as a marketing term and to indicate "an absence of positive connotations to the present" (74). The resurgence of a concern with language and form over content gives rise to a "climate" that Calabrese labels "neobaroque" and whose most salient trait is the use of "formal research" to fill the void left by the loss of "wholeness, globality, and systematicity" (vi). The writer Sebastiano Vassalli satirizes this tendency in his *Neo-italiano*. He describes the "neobaroque" as the "dominant esthetic during the banal 1980s," and as the "nonstyle" (characterized by *citazionismo* [the overriding use of quotations]) of the writer "who is not his own contemporary." In Vassalli's words, "unable to participate in his own life (even while living it) and unable to speak his own words (even while pronouncing them)," "neobaroque man" "has no choice but to repeat himself and others, who in turn are condemned to repeat what he has already said" (23, 77).

29. While meditating on her youth she uses the archaic *giovinezza*, title of the anthem of the Italian National Fascist Party and a term indicative of an important aspect of Fascist ideology. Lazzari argues that in the broad context of the "generic irrationalism that molds Fascist ideology and its language," the specific semantic area he labels "vitalistic" connotes a "certain philosophical conception . . . that privileges humanity's instinctive gifts, its creative energy, talent, and youth over maturity and intelligence, that praises the act of will at the expense of contemplative thought." He goes on to explain that "the word *giovinezza* [is] taken as a . . . cornerstone of that system of belief" (19).

30. This is an issue for Italian writers, many of whom (unlike Tabucchi who intentionally avoids television interviewers [Pivetta]) have made themselves available to the potentially corrupting influence of the small screen, willfully establishing themselves as "ubiquitous" "diva-istic" media "presences" (Costanzo quoted by Paternostro in Delfino *Rime scelte* 21–22).

31. The reference to Walter Benjamin is all too obvious.

32. Gadda's dialogue begins with the following declaration: "He who imagines and perceives himself as an isolated being carries the concept of individualism to the limits of negation; he dis-

torts it to the point of nullifying its content. . . . If a dragonfly goes to Tokyo, it sets off a chain reaction that involves me" (234).

33. The debunking of such hypocrisy is consistent with Tabucchi's views on the sociological phenomenon of the *pentiti*. As he told an interviewer, in the novella "Il battere d'ali" he ponders the issue of repentence (*il pentimento*). "It does not refer," he says, to a specific case, but to a general reality that we would do well without. It disturbs me because . . . repentance could be authentic but only if it foresaw expiation, if it coincides with the acknowledgment of responsibility for one's own actions" (Décina Lombardi). Instead, the driving forces behind Butterfly's decision to become a police informant are those of eluding responsibility and of petty vengeance on those who turned a deaf ear to his retorsions (see 86–87). The theme of "repentance" is central to Tabucchi's *Sostiene Pereira* where its connotation is positive. As the author has explained, in this work the term has no religious overtone. For Pereira it is a means of atonement for never having distanced himself from the past and for never having renewed himself spiritually or intellectually. When this does occur he is "reborn to a new life" and begins to "frequent the future" (see Petri 70–71).

34. The *I* of "La trota" reiterates the hypocritical lexicon of the confessional utilized by Butterfly. The former wishes to be "absolved" prior to composing a satire of his own work and asking an admirer to publish this and nineteen other madrigals after his death. In his words, "it was just grand, to be absolved and to sin, instead of sinning first and then seeking absolution, because absolution must come before the sin, sin must be preceded by absolution, by a preventive forgiving" (105). Given the immanent narrator's resemblance to Montale, this passagae is laden with intertextual irony. The lesson of Guido and Buonconte da Montefeltro (*Inf*. XXVII and *Purg*. V) would not have eluded the Nobel laureate, known for his Dantesque *rime petrose*.

Afterword

1. Perhaps the most significant example in recent memory is the manner in which the vast majority of Americans viewed the

Simpson murder trial: as a real-life soap opera. The trial gave cause, but only briefly, to reflect on the state of justice in America. The LAPD's conduct was not seen as the most evident manifestation of a nationwide phenomenon. Also silenced were the issues of the wealthy's unequal access to the legal system, and the importance for society at large to discuss the greater repercussions of the lack—within a specific microcosm, the LAPD crime laboratory—of a serious, professional work ethic.

2. Wolf contests what for Vattimo is the "necessary" transparence of mediatized society by citing glaring examples of opacity and distortion of factual reality in the media (*Gli effetti sociali dei media* 166). He also refutes Vattimo's contention that the self-awareness of mediatized societies of their own historical relativity, brought about by the electronic media, exposes to them the relativity of their "pretense of dominion." Wolf argues that by making visible hidden areas of the social world, the exceptions to the rule as it were, the media in effect reconfirms a society's beliefs about itself.

3. According to Wolf, television reports tendencies within society as it does hard news. These trends—not the underlying processes they reflect—form the basis of television's discourse on social reality ("The Evolution of Television Language in Italy" 292). The media give impetus to trends by giving them "visibility." Then, once mediatized, or presented as an expanding aspect of "public opinion," they become a point of reference for the public at large. They self-perpetuate, finding supporters among those who are led to adapt their views to what is perceived as potentially a majority viewpoint (*Gli effetti sociali* 71). In this way, television's nonanalytical "exposure" of "public opinion" becomes a self-fulfilling prophesy: so-called mainstream opinions become normative and dissent is ostracized. Media discussion of "public opinion," Wolf explains, through tacit coercion encourages conformity of thought and behavior because it threatens the dissenter with isolation and the politician with loss of popular support. Moreover, individuals convinced by media silence that their opinions are unique, abstain from expressing their views "for fear of violating a moral taboo or an authoritative rule or in order to avoid unpopularity" (74).

4. As Ferretti has pointed out, the conclusion of *Il nome della rosa* problematically overturns conventional detective-story structures with the victorious self-destruction of the assassin and the self-criticism of the investigator who fails to solve the case. Nonetheless, chaos (as Eco foresaw in theoretical writings that antedate his novel) is dominated and a new order installed (*Il best seller* 36).

5. It is ironic that Calvino's fellow metafictionist would assign to literature a role denounced by his mentor, Vittorini, during the postwar period. See Barth's novella "*Dunyazadiad.*" "If [the treasury of art] could not redeem the barbarities of history or spare us the horrors of living and dying, at least [it] sustained, refreshed, expanded, ennobled, and enriched our spirits along the painful way" (*Chimera* 17).

6. As Eco makes clear (perhaps in spite of himself) in the "Postille al *Nome della rosa,*" he as author identifies with his text. "I wanted, with all my strength," he writes, "to sketch the outline of a reader who, after having been initiated, became my prey, that is, the text's prey" (523).

Works Cited

Ahern, John. "Out of Montale's Cavern: A Reading of Calvino's *Gli amori difficili*," *Modern Language Studies* 12 (1982): 3–19.

Angelo, Bonnie. "The Pain of Being Black," interview with Toni Morrison. *Time* 22 May 1989, 120–22.

Approaching Postmodernism. Ed. Douwe Fokkema and Hans Bertens. Amsterdam/Philadelphia: John Benjamins Publishing Company, 1986. V. 21 in Utrecht Publications in General and Comparative Literature.

Asor Rosa, Alberto. "Lo Stato democratico e i partiti," *Il letterato e le istituzioni*; volume 1 of 9-volume *Letteratura italiana*. Ed. Alberto Asor Rosa. Turin: Einaudi, 1982, 549–643.

Barth, John. *The Friday Book. Essays and Other Non-fiction*. New York: Putnam, 1984.

———. *Chimera*. New York: Random House, 1972.

———. *Once Upon a Time. A Floating Opera*. Boston: Little, Brown and Company, 1994.

Barthes, Roland. *Barthes: Selected Writings*, 1982. Ed. Susan Sontag. London: Fontana/Collins, 1983.

———. "The Surrealists Overlooked the Body," in *The Grain of the Voice. Interviews 1962–1980*. Trans. Linda Coverdale. New York: Hill and Wang, 1985.

Bauman, Zygmunt. "Is There a Postmodern Sociology?" *Theory, Culture and Society*, 5 (1988): 217–37.

Belfiori, Giovanni. "Tabucchi: uno scrittore deve essere anche un buon ascoltatore," *La Gazzetta di Pesaro*, 12 July 1992.

Benjamin, Walter. *Illuminations*, 1955. New York: Harcourt, Brace and World, 1988.

Bennett, Tony. *Outside Literature*. London and New York: Routledge, 1990.

Binni, Walter. *Poetica, critica e storia letteraria e altri scritti di metodologia*. Florence: Casa editrice Le lettere, 1993.

Black Women Writers (1950–1980). A Critical Evaluation. Ed. Mari Evans. New York: Anchor Books, 1984.

Black Women Writers at Work. Ed. Claudia Tate. Harpenden, England: Oldcastle Books, 1983.

Blanchot, Maurice. *The Space of Literature*. Originally published in France as *L'Espace littéraire* in 1955. Translated, with an Introduction, by Ann Smock. Lincoln, NE: University of Nebraska Press, 1982.

Bonito Oliva, Achille. "Il linguaggio come comportamento mancato: il senso di colpa, la morte, il suicidio," in *Studi sul surrealismo*, 104–20.

Bono, Paola, and Sandra Kemp. "Coming from the South," in *Italian Feminist Thought*, 1–29.

Borges, Jorge Luis, *Ficciones*. 1956. Edited and with an Introduction by Anthony Kerrigan. New York: Grove Press, 1962.

———. *Labyrinths. Selected Stories & Other Writings*, Edited by Donald A. Yates and James E. Irby. Preface by André Maurois, 1962. New York: New Directions, 1964.

Borges, Jorge Luis, and Margarita Guerriero. *Manual de zoología fantástica*. Mexico City and Buenos Aires: Fondo de cultura económica, 1957.

Borsari, Andrea. "Cos'è una vita se non viene raccontata? Conversazione con Antonio Tabucchi," *Italienisch—Zeitschrift für Italienische Sprache und Literatur*, November 1991, 2–23.

Caesar, Michael. "Italian Fiction in the Nineteen-Eighties," in *Postmodernism and Contemporary Fiction*. Ed. E.J. Smith. London: B.T. Batsford, 1991, 74–89.

Calabrese, Omar. *L'età neobarocca*. 1987. Rome-Bari: Laterza, 1992.

Calvino, Italo. *Il sentiero dei nidi di ragno*, 1947. Turin: Einaudi, 1964.

———. "*Introduzione*," in Calvino, *Fiabe italiane*, 1956, v. 1. Milan: Mondadori, 1991, IX–LI.

———. *Gli amori difficili*, 1958. Turin: Einaudi, 1973.

———. *Le cosmicomiche*. Turin: Einaudi, 1965.

———. *Ti con zero*. Turin: Einaudi, 1967.

———. *La memoria del mondo e altre storie cosmicomiche*, 1968. Ed. Giulio Bollati. Turin: Einaudi, 1975.

———. "Chi cattura chi?" L'approdo letterario, January–March 1968, pp. 105–10.

———. "I segni alti," in Melotti, *Lo spazio inquieto*, 91–92.

———. *Le città invisibili*. Turin: Einaudi: 1972.

———. *Il castello dei destini incrociati*. Turin: Einaudi, 1973.

———. "Autobiografia di uno spettatore," in Federico Fellini, *Quattro film*. Turin: Einaudi, 1974.

———. "La squadratura," in Giulio Paolini, *Idem* Turin: Einaudi, 1975. VII–XIV.

———. "Forse un mattino andando," in *Letture montaliane. In occasione dell'ottantesimo compleanno del poeta*. Genoa: Bozzi, 1977.

———. *Se una notte d'inverno un viaggiatore*. Turin: Einaudi, 1979.

———. "Sono stato stalinista anch'io?," *Repubblica*, 16–17 December 1979.

———. "L'etnologo bifronte," *Repubblica*, 6 August 1980, 12.

———. *Una pietra sopra. Discorsi di letteratura e società*. Turin: Einaudi, 1980.

———. "Quel giorno i carri armati uccisero le nostre speranze," *Repubblica*, 13 December 1980.

———. "Prose and Anticombinatorics," 1981, in *Oulipo. A Primer of Potential Literature*, 143–52.

———. "The Written and the Unwritten Word," *New York Review of Books*, 12 May 1983.

———. *Palomar*, 1983. Milan: Mondadori, 1990.

———. *Cosmicomiche vecchie e nuove*. Milan: Garzanti, 1984.

———. *Collezione di sabbia*, 1984. Milan: Bompiani, 1990.

———. "La mia città è New York," in *Mal d'America*, 157–62.

———. *Sotto il sole giaguaro*. Milan: Bompiani, 1992.

———. *Lezioni americane. Sei proposte per il prossimo millennio*. Milan: Mondadori, 1993.

Calvino Revisited. Ed. Franco Ricci. University of Toronto Italian Studies 2. Ottawa: Dovehouse Editions, 1989.

Camon, Ferdinando. *Il mestiere di scrittore*. Milan: Garzanti, 1973.

Cannon, JoAnn. *Postmodern Italian Fiction. The Crisis of Reason in Calvino, Eco, Sciascia, Malerba*. Rutherford, N.J.: Farleigh Dickinson Univeristy Press, 1989.

———. "Italo Calvino: The Last Two Decades," in *Calvino Revisited*, 51–64.

Carabi, Angels. Interview with Toni Morrison, *Belles lettres*, v.9n.3, 1994, 38–39,86–90.

Ceserani, Remo. "Modernity and Postmodernity: A Cultural Change Seen from the Italian Perspective." *Italica*, 71 (1994): 369–84.

Cigliana, Simona. "Il lavoro dello scrittore." *Il cavallo di Troia*, June 1986, 7–13+.

Corti, Maria. "Intervista: Italo Calvino." *Autografo*, 2 (1985): 47–53.

Costanzo, Mario. *Appunti e postille per un Seminario di Storia della critica letteraria*. Rome: Bulzoni, 1991.

Critical Essays on Toni Morrison. Ed. Nellie Y. McKay. Boston: G.K. Hall, 1988.

Darling, Marsha. "In the Realm of Responsibility," interview with Toni Morrison. *The Women's Review of Books*, March 1988. 6–7.

Décina Lombardi, Paola. "Tabucchi in nero," *Tuttolibri*, 2 March 1991, 3.

Delfino, Giovanni. *Rime scelte*. Edited by Mario Costanzo. Introduction by Rocco Paternostro (pp. 7–30). Rome: Bulzoni, 1995.

d'Eramo, Marco. "Nel corso di una vita. Italo Calvino" (interview). *Mondoperaio*. v. 32 (1979), n.6 (June), pp. 133–38.

Doctorow, E.L. "Ragtime Revisited," *Neiman Reports* Summer–Autumn 1977, 3–8+

———. "Living in the House of Fiction," *The Nation*, 22 April, 1978, 459–62.

———. "Creators on Creating," *Saturday Review*, October 1980, 44–48.

———. "A Spirit of Transgression," in *E.L. Doctorow. Essays and Conversations*, 31–47.

———. "The Writer as Independent Witness," in *E.L. Doctorow. Essays and Conversations*, 58–69.

———. "Fiction is a System of Knowledge," *Michigan Quarterly Review*, 30 (1991): 439–56.

———. *Jack London, Hemingway, and the Constitution. Selected Essays, 1977–1992*. New York: Random House, 1993.

———. *The Waterworks*. New York: Random House, 1994.

Dombroski, Robert S. *Antonio Gramsci*. Boston: Twayne Publishers, 1989.

———. *Properties of Writing. Ideological Discourse in Modern Italian Fiction.* Baltimore: Johns Hopkins Univeristy Press, 1994.

Ebert, Teresa L. "The 'Difference' of Postmodern Feminism," *College English*, 53 (1991): 886–904.

Eco, Umberto. *Lector in fabula. La cooperazione nei testi narrativi*. Milan: Bompiani, 1979.

———. *Il nome della rosa*, 1980. Milan: Bompiani, 1993.

———. "Intentio lectoris: The State of the Art," in *Recoding Metaphysics*, 27–43.

Edwards, Brian. "Deconstructing the Artist and the Art: Barth and Calvino at Play in the Funhouse of Language," *Canadian Review of Comparative Literature*, June 1985, 264–86.

E.L. Doctorow. Essays and Conversations. Ed. Richard Trenner. Princeton: Ontario Review Press, 1983.

Federman, Raymond. "Surfiction—Four Propositions in Form of an Introduction," in Federman, *Surfiction. Fiction Now and Tomorrow*. Chicago: Swallow Press, 1972, 5–15.

———. *Critifiction. Postmodern Essays*. Albany: SUNY Press, 1993.

Feminist Criticism: Theory and Practice. Ed. Susan Sellers. New York: Harvester Wheatsheaf, 1991.

Ferguson, Rebecca. "History, Memory and Language in Toni Morrison's *Beloved*," in *Feminist Criticism*, 109–27.

Ferretti, Gian Carlo. *Il best seller all'italiana*, 1983. Milan: Masson, 1993.

———. *Le capre di Bikini. Calvino giornalista e saggista 1945–1985*. Rome: Editori Riuniti, 1989.

———. *Il mercato delle lettere*. Milan: Il Saggiatore, 1994.

Foster, Hal. *Compulsive Beauty*. Cambridge: MIT Press, 1993.

Francese, Joseph. "Tabucchi: una conversazione plurivoca," *Spunti e ricerche*, 6 (1990): 19–34.

———. "L'eteronimia di Antonio Tabucchi," *Stanford Italian Review*, 11 (1992) 123–38.

———. "The Postmodern Discourses of Doctorow's *Billy Bathgate* and Tabucchi's *Dialoghi mancati*," *Annali d'italianistica* 9 (1991): 182–97.

Freud, Sigmund. *A General Introduction to Psychoanalysis*. Trans. Joan Riviere. New York: Simon and Schuster, 1963.

Frye, Northrop. *Anatomy of Criticism*. Princeton: Princeton University Press, 1957.

Gadda, Carlo Emilio. *I viaggi, la morte*, 1958. Milan: Garzanti, 1977.

Gramsci, Antonio. *Quaderni del carcere*, 1975. Ed. Valentino Gerratana. Turin: Einaudi, 1977.

Harvey, David. *The Condition of Postmodernity. An Enquiry into the Origins of Cultural Change*. Cambridge, Mass: Basil Blackwell, 1989.

Hayles, N. Katherine. *Chaos Bound. Orderly Disorder in Contemporary Literature and Science*. Ithaca: Cornell University Press, 1990.

Herman, David, J. "Modernism versus Postmodernism. Towards an Analytic Distinction." *Poetics Today*, 12 (1991): 55–86.

Hutcheon, Linda. "Metafictional Implications for Novelistic Reference," in *On Referring in Literature*, 1–13.

Italian Feminist Thought. A Reader. Ed. Paola Bono and Sandra Kemp. Oxford: Basil Blackford, 1991.

Italo Calvino. Videotheque: The Great Twentieth Century Writers. Hanover, N.H.: Editiones del Norte.

Jameson, Frederic. *The Seeds of Time*. New York: Columbia University Press, 1994.

Kuhn, Thomas S. *The Structure of Scientific Revolutions*, 1962. Chicago: University of Chicago Press, 1970.

La Porta, L., and M. Sinibaldi. "Ultime leve," *Linea d'ombra*, 1984, n.7, 89–95.

Lazzari, Giovanni. *Le parole del fascismo*. Rome: Argileto, 1975.

Lemon, Lee T., and Marion J. Reis. *Russian Formalist Criticism. Four Essays*. Translated with an Introduction by Lemon and Reis. Lincoln: University of Nebraska Press, 1965.

Lester, Rosemarie K. "An Interview with Toni Morrison," in *Critical Essays on Toni Morrison*, 47–54.

Letteratura e arti figurative. Ed. Antonio Franceschetti. Florence, 1988.

Leube, Eberhard. "Sul rapporto tra letteratura e arti figurative nelle ultime opere di Italo Calvino," in *Letteratura e arti figurative*, vol. III, 1201–9.

Literature and the American Urban Experience. Ed. Michael C. Jaye and Ann Chalmers Watt. New Brunswick: Rutgers University Press, 1981.

Lucente, Gregory. "An Interview with Italo Calvino." *Contemporary Literature*, 26 (1985): 245–53.

Luperini, Romano. *Il novecento: apparati ideologici, ceto intellettuale, sistemi formali nella letteratura italiana contemporanea*. Turin: Loescher, 1981.

Mal d'America. Ed. Ugo Rubeo. Rome: Editori Riuniti, 1987.

Manacorda, Giuliano. *Letteratura italiana d'oggi. 1965–1985*. Rome: Editori Riuniti, 1987.

Mattei, Paolo. "Gli angeli neri che abitano il nostro tempo," *Il Tempo*, 10 April 1991, 8.

Mauro, Walter. "Calvino al crocevia fra realtà e favola." *Il Tempo*, 20 February, 1984, p. 3.

McKay, Nellie. "An Interview with Toni Morrison," *Contemporary Literature*, 24 (1983): 413–29.

Melotti, Fausto. *Lo spazio inquieto*. Ed. Paolo Fossati. Turin: Einaudi, 1971.

Merleau-Ponty, Jean Jacques Maurice. *Phenomenology of Perception*, 1962. Trans. Colin Smith. London: Routledge & Kegan Paul, 1979.

Mitchell, W.J.T. "Ekphrasis and the Other," *South Atlantic Quarterly* 91 (1992): 695–719.

Moderno postmoderno. Soggetto, tempo, sapere nella società attuale. Ed. Giovanni Mari. Milan: Feltrinelli, 1987.

Montale, Eugenio. *L'opera in versi*. Ed. Rosanna Bettarini and Gianfranco Contini. Turin: Einaudi, 1980.

Morrison, Toni. "City Limits, Village Values: Concepts of the Neighborhood in Black Fiction," in *Literature and the American Urban Experience*, 35–43.

———. Interview in *Black Women Writers at Work*, 117–31.

———. "Rootedness: The Ancestor as Foundation," in *Black Women Writers (1950–1980)*, 339–45.

———. "Memory, Creation, and Writing," *Thought*, 59 (1984): 385–90.

———. *Beloved*. 1987. New York: New American Library, 1988.

———. "Living Memory." *City Limits*, March 31—April 7, 1988, 10–11.

———. "Unspeakable Things Unspoken: The Afro-American Presence in American Literature," *Michigan Quarterly Review*, 28 (1989) 1–34.

———. *Playing in the Dark. Whiteness and the Literary Imagination*. Cambridge, Mass.: Harvard University Press: 1990.

———. "Friday on the Potomac," in *Race-ing Justice, En-gendering Power*, vii–xxx.

Motte Jr., Warren F. "Telling Games," in *Calvino Revisited*, 117–30.

Musarra, Ulla. "Duplication and Multiplication: Postmodernist Devices in the Novels of Italo Calvino," in *Approaching Postmodernism*, 135–55.

Nascimbeni, Giulio. "Sono un po' stanco di essere Calvino," *Corriere della sera*, 5 December 1984.

Naylor, Gloria, and Morrison, Toni. "A Conversation," *The Southern Review*, 21 (1991): 567–93.

On Referring in Literature. Ed. Anna Whiteside and Michael Issacharoff. Bloomington: Indiana University Press, 1987.

Oulipo. A Primer of Potential Literature. Ed. Warren F. Motte Jr. Lincoln: University of Nebraska Press, 1986.

Paternostro, Rocco. *Poetica dell'assenza*. Rome: Bulzoni, 1990.

———. "I perché degli incontri," in *Sotto la Torre*, 11–17.

———. Introduction to Delfino.

Pessoa, Fernando. *Obras completa de Fernando Pessoa*, 1952, 11 vols. 2nd. ed. Lisbon: Àtica, 1964–67.

Petri, Romana. "Uno scrittore pieno di gente," *Leggere*, June 1994, 68–75.

Pivetta, Oreste. "Quadri in rivolta," *l'Unità*, 27 September 1993.

Race-ing Justice, En-gendering Power. Essays on Anita Hill, Clarence Thomas, and the Construction of Social Reality. Ed. Toni Morrison. New York: Pantheon, 1992.

Ramondino, Fabrizia. "Il mondo incantato del signor 'Palomar,'" *Il mattino*, 8 January 1984.

Recoding Metaphysics. The New Italian Philosophy. Ed. Giovanna Borradori. Evanston, Ill: Northwestern University Press, 1988.

Ricci, Franco. "Painting with Words, Writing with Pictures," in *Calvino Revisited*, 189–206.

Rubenstein, Roberta. *Boundaries of Self. Gender, Culture, Fiction*. Urbana: University of Illinois Press, 1987.

"Scrittori d'Italia," *Espresso*, 12 January 1986, 80–86.

Simpson, David. *The Academic Postmodern and the Rule of Literature. A Report on Half-Knowledge*. Chicago: University of Chicago Press, 1995.

Smart, Robert Augustin. *The Nonfiction Novel*. Lanham, Md., and London: University Press of America, 1985.

Sotto la Torre. Incontri sulla letteratura italiana dell'Otto–Novecento. Ed. Rocco Paternostro. Rome: La Fenice, 1993.

Studi sul surrealismo, Rome: Officini Edizioni, 1977.

Tabucchi, Antonio. *La parola interdetta. Poeti surrealisti portoghesi*. Turin: Einaudi, 1971.

———. *Piazza d'Italia*. Milan: Bompiani, 1975.

———. *Il piccolo naviglio*. Milan: Mondadori, 1978.

———. "Àlvaro de Campos e Zeno Cosini: due coscienze parallele," *Studi filologici e letterari dell'Istituto di filologia romanza e ispanistica dell'Università di Genova*. Genoa: Bozzi, 1978. 151–62.

———. *Notturno indiano*. Palermo: Sellerio, 1984.

———. *Piccoli equivoci senza importanza*. Milan: Feltrinelli, 1985.

———. "Equivoci senza importanza," *Mondoperaio*, n. 12, 1985, 109–11.

———. *Il filo dell'orizzonte*. Milan: Feltrinelli, 1986.

———. *I volatili del Beato Angelico*. Palermo: Sellerio, 1987.

———. *Un baule pieno di gente. Scritti su Fernando Pessoa*. Milan: Feltrinelli, 1990.

———. "Some Reflections on Translation." Paper read at a conference organized by the Ministry of Arts of Victoria, Australia, in 1991.

———. *L'angelo nero*. Milan: Feltinelli, 1991.

———. *Requiem, uma alucinação*. 1991. Italian trans., Sergio Vecchio. Milan: Feltrinelli, 1991.

———. *Sostiene Pereira. Una testimonianza*. Milan: Feltrinelli, 1994.

Tornabuoni, Lietta. "Calvino, l'occhio e il silenzio," *La stampa*, 25 November 1983, 3.

Trenner, Richard. "Politics and the Mode of Fiction," in *E.L. Doctorow. Essays and Conversations*, 48–56.

Vassalli, Sebastiano. *Il neo-italiano. Le parole degli anni ottanta*. Bologna: Zanichelli, 1989.

Vattimo, Gianni. *La società trasparente*. Milan: Garzanti, 1989.

———. "*Postmoderno, tecnologia, ontologia*," *Micro-Mega*, n. 4, 1990, 83–95.

———. "*Postmodernità e fine della storia*," in *Moderno postmoderno*, 98–108.

White, Hayden. *The Content of the Form: Narrative Discourse and Historical Representation*. Baltimore: Johns Hopkins University Press, 1987.

———. "Getting Out of History," *Diacritics*, 12 (fall 1982): 2–13.

Wolf, Mauro. "The Evolution of Television Language in Italy since Deregulation, in *Culture and Conflict in Postwar Italy*. Ed. Zygmunt G. Baranski and Robert Lumley. New York: St. Martin's Press, 1990, 286–94.

———. *Gli effetti sociali dei media*. Milan: Bompiani, 1992.

Index